Biggin Hill Airfield
Beyond the Bump I
By

Joseph J. Merchant
Including
Contributions

from former Biggin Hill Flight Instructors:

Mick Ronayne
&
Bob Needham

Publisher

Pilots Pals
Springfields, Kings Bank Lane,
Beckley, East Sussex. TN31 6RU
England

Printer
CreateSpace

Front Cover photo: Via Mick Ronayne "Spirit of Biggin"

Cover Design by Kate O'Shaughnessy

ISBN 978-0-9929626-0-9

Dedicated to:

My loving Sister Rosemary and my
devoted Brother-in-Law Philip

For their encouragement and support.

Contents "Beyond the Bump I"

Beyond the Bump II

Plans are to publish volume II of my work during 2015, it will be in full colour recalling my days of turning hobbies into my income. Aviation, glamour photography and parties.

The Author

Who is Joe Merchant? A question asked many times by all sorts of people, including Bromley Borough Council and the Clacton Home for the Bewildered. Maybe the following will help answer it.

I first met Joe at 150 ft. on the approach to Biggin Hill on a sunny day in 1965. He was flying a Chipmunk and I was in a venerable old Auster V and we were both vying to land on the same grass runway! Being non-radio, we were both shouting at each other - a pointless effort, given that neither would have heard the other, Joe won, turning inside me for final approach. Our association began then and has continued around many of the clubs on Biggin Hill and other less salubrious places. When we 'met', I was working as a young journalist on Flight magazine flying at weekends with the Experimental Flying Group and Joe was equally keen as a member of 600 City of London Flying Group. Our common interest in aviation kept us together as friends during the glory days of Biggin Hill and with other colleagues we flew and laughed our way through those heady days which remain our most enjoyable . Joe is a complex character, as we all are to a greater or lesser degree. He always seems to have rushed about everywhere at full speed and maybe my rather laid back approach to certain aspects of life have led him to wonder how I managed to get things done at all.

Joe is obsessive and wherever he has lived, his garden is a picture of order and tidiness - the grass was finely cut, weeds were a rarity and woe betides anyone who dares to tread on any part of the garden that wasn't a dedicated pathway; the result of being given a lawn mower at six months old. Where he lives in Spain, a country not know for the finely-honed gardens of England. Joe has addressed 50 ft-high palms and threatened them with extinction if they so much as shed a frond without his explicit agreement.

Joe is good company, a factor that made his clubs on Biggin Hill such a success. At the air shows, Pilots Pals was the watering hole for a host of international participants from across Europe, producing a sort of miniature United Nations of aviation. If you were a pilot and loved aviation, the common theme was enjoyment and endless discussions about flying, aerobatics, beer and women! Mentioning women, the fairer sex has played a big part of in Joe's life and if Valerie, his wife, will forgive me, his Pilot's Pals became part of the Biggin Hill scene through the 1980s and 90s. Not everyone thought the Pals were appropriate, but they were harmless and brightened up the lives of the many flyers, particularly those serving with 56 Squadron, R.A.F. with whom Joe had a close relationship going back to his Air Training Corps days. Unforgettable, was the look of incredulity on the faces of the young American sailors aboard the USS Forrestal when Joe pitched up on the flight deck with a handful of glamorous, white booted girls and asked if they could drape themselves over some the jets for a few pictures! These images he used for the production of his well-known calendar and flight safety posters.

His many Pilot's Pals and friends were a great support during his ambitious ventures that included hanger dances and private fly-pasts; mounted for almost any reason but all aimed at maintaining the spirit of Biggin Hill. His most ambitious project was, with approval of the Station Commander to organise the fly past on the closure of R.A.F. Biggin Hill. He had a life-long dedication to our armed services and their charities. To this end he organised an annual "Old Soldiers Day" whereby the private owners and club members gave their guests, who included Chelsea Pensioners, Parachute Regimen, Royal Navy and Royal Air Force the experience of private flying. All ex-service men and women were made welcome, fed and watered by him.

Joe has two sons, Gary and Roy, the former currently flying the unwashed to southern Europe aboard orange-coloured Airbuses, while Roy opted for the more artistic style of life. Both do him great credit.

This book gives you a snapshot of Joe's life on Biggin Hill and many of the people who have helped shape it. While it hasn't all been beer and skittles, we have both survived and will remain good friends to the end, when the cry will go up *'Time Gentlemen, Please'!*

Barry C. Wheeler

Biggin Hill Airfield
Beyond the Bump I
By
Joseph J Merchant

My association with 56 Sqn. R.A.F. was a long and happy one.
Note my number plate.

This is the true story of my funny life as a young and not so young dreamer. My enthusiasm for aviation took me to the most famous fighter station in the world, fulfilling my dreams with endless riches of reality, flying, Guinness and beautiful women.

By walking in the footsteps of my aviation heroes, sharing the humour of so many other pilots and friends, I regard myself as one of the most fortunate humans of our time having spent 53 years at R.A.F. Biggin Hill, affectionately known as the "Bump" and latterly Biggin Hill Airport.

Welcome to my wonderful world of aviation.

Chapter 1

Life is a gift to enjoy. From an early age my enthusiasm for nature; its plants, flowers and animals all played their part in overcoming the inevitable strained events of this gift. I never questioned these simple pleasures knowing it was all within reach, but suddenly it was all taken away. However, my thoughts were that one-day I would again walk in green fields, smell the wild roses and brush both hands on oaks. My enduring thirst for aviation, gained as a young boy, was to bring all these desires to fruition once I found Biggin Hill.

Joseph J. Merchant 1986

Chapter One

The big day had arrived for Mum and Dad, 7th May 1940, delivering me into the 'phoney war'. Three days later the Germans offensive started in earnest and hard on its heels came Dunkirk, the "Battle of France" lost and the "Battle of Britain" looming. July saw the start of the non-contractual demolition job by our mates the Germans. These days were known as "The Dark Days" well they were for me I couldn't see a bloody thing of what must have been Europe's greatest air show. (I had to wait for the film.) Many of our boys and girls paid the ultimate price defending our freedom. God bless them all. One thing is for sure this period had a great influence in developing my passion for aviation.

My birthplace was Greenwich, South East London. Greenwich hospital was then situated just a gnat's whisker west of the Meridian line. No that's not a shipping company, it is the imaginary line of longitude that circles our planet as a navigation aid. The Prime Meridian, Zero degrees, passes through Greenwich while on the other side of the world, at 180 Degrees; it is called the International Date Line. Greenwich is one hell of a place to be born, at Zero. I had something in common with Greenwich but still waiting to leave hospital. Things were looking up!

My Christian name came from within the family, Uncle Joseph. What a chap he must have been. Apparently one evening he went from his home in North Woolwich travelled to South Woolwich, got himself severely drunk and on his return journey home he threw himself off the Woolwich Free Ferry. Shame! Later my Grandfather told me he fell in fooling around but Grandma said he was thirsty, who do you believe? However, Joseph it was to be after my very wet uncle. What happened next? The family home was bombed and I, along with thousands of other children, were evacuated to be dispersed around England for safekeeping. London must have been nappyless during those dark days. First stop of the evacuation was to Bleadon, Somerset, that's the name of a village. Next onto Sodden, Wales, that's another meaning for wet. Boy does it rain in Wales. I thought sunshine was a bank holiday.

During those early days at Bleadon my Dad took me to nearby Weston-super-Mare. On that visit I was to be introduced to my very first aircraft. The Royal Air Force had a *"Save for Victory"* collection point on the sea front *"Help Buy a Spitfire"*. Due to my continued insistence my Dad had me placed into the aircraft that proved to be a complete waste of time due to my

Chapter One

size, I was looking up at the control column within this very dark hole called the cockpit. Knobs, switches, levers and a smell, oh that smell, it hit me like an oncoming pram. I was in love, deeply and truly. Now you try explaining to the R.A.F. chaps that my Dad's sixpence had given me full rights to this aircraft, not thinking of how I was to get it home or, where to put it. It was to be all mine. Sadly I was forced to leave the aircraft and return to the normal life that I had left earlier on that special day. Those memories, that unforgettable smell, and oh the pain. Should anyone inform you that a child's emotions or childish fads are short lived and that one should ignore such feelings, their wrong. A child's constructive enthusiasm needs encouragement, commitment and patience for it to reap the opportunities in their future.

It came to my notice that I was not unique in the family, coming to terms with two older sisters, Jean being the eldest then Rosemary. This was somewhat of a challenge particularly at feeding time. Why was I always so hungry? Thinking back Mum must have coped well in feeding us, considering the hardship of rationing. I remember so well sharing an apple core with my sister Rosemary. Jean had the apple. Overall the family relationship was good fun continuously improving with time, it's called growing up. At an early age, the family bond was forged.

Moving from Bleadon, Somerset to Sodden Wales gave me endless views of the beautiful undulating county side of Glamorganshire. Here I was to find that veg grew upside down and the locals had reverse gear fitted to their speech. I was to learn new ways and things. I thought Wellington boots were part of the Welsh National Dress, boy did it rain. All this and the move softened the loss of my continuous longing for aircraft until one day I showed yet another enthusiastic gesture for aviation. My dear Mum was called to my nursery to explain where I had learned the use of bad language.
"What has he done now?" Asked my Mum.
Apparently during one of the infrequent air raids all the children in the school playground scattered for cover while I was seen and heard waving my fist shouting.
"You Bastards."
Yet another clip round the ear.

My appreciation of aromas at such an early age pleased me, not just the Spitfire cockpit, there were the wild roses on the railway embankment,

Chapter One

Scarlet Pimpernels, Wild Daffodils, Fox Gloves, and my favourite the Wild Primrose. These endless, yet simple, free pleasures seemed to fill my damp days. I was to learn the art of free food, scrumping, how funny that free food always tasted better than served food and yet had very different results the following day. I loved Mum's saying

"Too much of a good thing is bad for you."

What could a child say to follow that? Although I did think hard about Mum's statement. Rain is a good thing, it keeps one clean but don't go out in it too often, it's bad for you. What choice did we have living in sodden Wales? I was tall for my age at four, hence the constant comments from my relations.

"He's going to be a tall lad, bit skinny."

What did they expect with little sustenance followed by a daily watering? I resembled a piece of neglected Welsh Ivy.

Jean, my eldest sister, returned to London after winning a scholarship to the Woolwich Polytechnic. Further education was not available in South Wales at that time. The rest of the family would not join her until the war with Germany was over, Dad was employed on vital war work at the Royal Ordnance Factory, Bridgend. Our return was to take place as soon as possible after Victory in Europe. Leaving the beautiful green countryside of Wales and arriving at my Grandparents house in Silvertown, East London was a social shock to me. The smell of damp bombed housing was nauseating; this area, being so close to the London Docks, now City Airport had taken the worst of what Germany could deliver. I hated this environment; it was smelly, damp and dirty. The old house that gave me a feeling of loneliness, the first time that I had felt such a bad emotion. I was very sad; sadness brought the ever-increasing misery in the long days and nights.

August 1945 - Victory over Japan, the war was finally over! . It was in all the newspapers making many people happy. I remember that we had lots of bread and jam washed down with tap water. Flags were flying, people dancing in the streets to the now familiar sound of Glen Miller.. Only on special occasions can you do the happiness bits, have you noticed? Two countries have to knock seven colours of sugar out of each other. Then you get your celebration

My life continued as normal but living with my Grandparents was really awful. The local school gave me no confidence, in fact I was demoralised to such a point I wanted to run away. I was longing for the countryside just to walk on green grass, to smell the flowers and to see the wild life. However, Silvertown had no grass or wild life. I think most of these had been consumed by the local population. I was sad and lonely; and even when surrounded by others something was missing.

1946 - The council allocated us a home in Plumstead, S. E. London. Trees, grass, two commons for me to walk plus Shewsbury Park nearby. Things had started to improve. Dad had returned from Wales to find his old job waiting for him at Mum's uncle's transport company. Dad had been a drayman before the war, delivering beer to the East End of London, now he was delivering paint to the docks. That gave me opportunities to see the ships having their various cargoes unloaded. These ships, especially those that were both passenger and cargo vessels needed a lot of paint. Delivering the heavy loads relied on the sheer power of his trusted pair of Shire horses. Weekends and school holidays gave me the chance to join Dad either on deliveries or on a Saturday cleaning the stables and horses. There were three Shires in total, two working one resting. Saturdays had to be my favourite day, I loved feeding time, obviously they fed every day but on Saturdays they got a special treat, Hot water poured on the feed followed by a quart of Guinness; yes, Guinness. Dad assured me that Guinness was an essential part of their weekly diet.

"For pregnant women, old ladies and horses, Guinness was the answer."
Said Dad.
That was a downer; I didn't fall into any of the categories. However, I used to swig the remains from the bottle when Dad was not looking. Three years later I was to say goodbye to my now three beautiful friends. Dad was issued with a Austin Van and the three Shires went to a home in Essex for retired horses. The times I have driven past that farm thinking of my dear friends. A strange feeling of loneliness would return penetrating deep into my youth. However, I would think *Guinness'* and smile.

The family was happy in our new dwelling at 38 Genesta Road, Plumstead. S.E. London. We had fruit trees in the garden, an apple, a pear and a cherry, plus a large area for Dad's planned vegetable patch. This was essential to help feed us all. Dad's weekly wage packet was small. We were a poor family; food was almost a luxury and none was to be wasted. Leftovers provided the next meal, such as bubble and squeak, soups and the many other concoctions skilfully made by Mum. This lack of sustenance did not help my physique and yet, according to government statistics in 1944, the British population had never been so healthy. So, how was it I was so skinny? I decided Guinness was the answer; okay I was not old, pregnant or a horse, but seeing what my Dad's shires could do it had to work on me. Collecting empty beer bottles became a full time hobby, I would return the empties to recover the deposit paid on all bottled beers. Ten empties gave you a free pint. I hid the empties in the old building at the end of the garden until I reached my target. My journey to the off-licence was a little scary, what if Mum or Dad found out, they would think I was a potential alcoholic. I needed my Guinness! Returning to my hide-out clutching the famous brew, I opened the glass container with excitement thinking this time tomorrow I shall take on Super Man. Two hours later the only thing that had increased in size was my head. I confessed to Mum why, and what I had done hoping she could help me in some way. Understanding as she was I found myself, with Mum, first in our doctor's surgery and from there to hospital for a check up. A huge man who was sneezing, sputtering and coughing during the whole of the embarrassing examination prodded me in ever possible part of my anatomy. I couldn't resist saying to him.

"I think you should see a doctor about that cold."
Mum went absolutely mental smacking me across the legs, but that was after the now laughing big guy agreed with me. Still coughing and laughing he recommended I have a X-ray on my chest. Passing my file to the nurse he said

"Don't waste time using the machine, just hold him up to a 60 watt bulb and you will get an instant reading."
I was thin, so bad I couldn't get a suntan because the rays missed me. I wanted to do body building but I didn't have a body to build anything on.

"Empty your pockets." Cried Mum.
My pockets were empty it was me that was rattling.

1950's - Life improved with an addition to our family when Dad had purchased our first dog, Mickey, a cross Labrador/ Alsatian. That dog filled my life with so many happy hours. In reality it gave me responsibilities to take care of him, ensuring he was fed at the correct time, brushed and cleaned.

For the school summer holidays Mum and Dad had agreed to send me to relations who lived in the country, this was to build me up I was told. Back to the country, great. The memories of flowers, animals and green fields rushed through my mind. However, both Uncle Len and Aunty Ginny

Chapter One

worked all week and I would have to be a good boy. In other words I would have to look after myself, fine I thought. Finding out exactly where they lived and what sort of factory they both worked in knocked me back. Their home was in the village of Highworth near Swindon and their factory, Vickers. What did Vickers build? Aircraft, jet aircraft. Until my departure I don't think I slept one single night through. The great day had arrived, Mum and I set off catching a bus to London then the train to Swindon. The journey from Swindon to Highworth was very exciting. My nose constantly pressed on the bus window hoping to catch a view of the Vickers factory. Suddenly the airfield appeared; three jets on a hard standing with people in white overalls standing around one of them. I would have 6 weeks of this, what more could a child want.

The endless sunny days gave me views of Mike Lithgo and other test pilots putting their new machines through the test programmes. These were explained to me by Uncle Len. For me it was sheer heaven. If I was not at the factory fence I would go horse riding, and I would still be able to see the condensation trails of those lucky flyers. God, how I wanted to fly but it was fun on the back of a horse. I never, in my life, had a riding lesson, hence the reason, why I kept falling off. I recall the last day of my holiday, not much happening at Vickers so back to the stables for a last ride before returning to my council tip. Paying my shilling to the yard boy, grabbed my favourite horse, got on, no saddle, the only thing that the horse would wear was the reins and its silly grin that amused me. Off I went into the green county side of Wiltshire occasionally hearing the jets pushing the sound barrier. It was pure poetry, music to my ears, the warm breast of a Mother. I was so happy and as young as I was I was going to live in the country and fly. I had identified and found what was missing in my life. All well and said but how?
I fancied a gallop before returning to the tip, home. Off I fell straight into the biggest cow-pat you have ever seen, if nothing else the amount helped break the fall. I was covered from right shoulder to my knees in fresh cow shit. Off went my horse jumping into the next field that contained one ugly fully grown bull. Now, picture the scene. The horse is looking at the bull, the bull was looking at me. Remember I'm covered in cow shit, the bull then looked at the horse, the horse looked at me, all heads were turning like a Swiss mechanism. At this stage of the horrendous predicament it became very obvious that there was some screwing to be done and it wasn't going to be me, so bullocks, I left the two individuals to sort out their own futures.

Chapter One

Before the war Mum, Dad together with other members of the family, Uncles, Aunt's and Cousins spent part of the summers going hop picking in Kent. You worked all day picking hops; this then gave you a shack, bed and inexpensive farm food. That was your holiday. However, times were changing; Mum and Dad had fallen in love with Margate in Kent during a day coach trip. They took me and my best schoolmate Ricky. Dad gave me ten shilling (50p) for my day's entertainment. Ricky had five shillings (25p). Mum and Dad went off to have their cockles, beer and sing "Knees up Mother Brown" As a boy, I took it that this was the formula for having their party time. Before leaving us to do our own thing, we received the usual instructions to be good boys and not to get up to any mischief. Off we went to explore this great British resort. The very first attraction was a signboard, JOY FLIGHTS 7/6d (37.5p) PER HEAD. Ricky, being Ricky cried out

"I want all of me to go."

The cost for the two of us was all that both of us had the for the entire day's entertainment; Being driven to the small grass strip just outside Margate we saw our aircraft, a de.H Rapide. The excitement was almost uncontrollable. I said very little to my partner trying so hard to absorb every second of this dream to come true. The aircraft taxied to the end of the field and immediately started to bump its way into the air, and suddenly I was flying. The coast line of Kent, the cotton wool clouds, the short fat girl opposite me throwing up in a makeshift vomitorium. (Aviation term for sick bag). This was flying! God I was happy. Those 15 minutes took me closer to my heaven confirming my desire to be involved with aviation. During this excitement I failed to note the registration of the aircraft, I would have loved to have monitored its journey through time.

I loved my first school camp. Wrens Warren, in the Ashdown Forest. Seven days back in the county, long walks as dawn broke, the plants, flower and animals thrilled me. Only in the early hours might you see a group of Rabbits bouncing their way to a better feeding place, or, in the distance across the valley a large herd of Deer. Yes, I was on my own; I had no need for company, selfish? No, I think I was too embarrassed to talk about such things to the other boys. I regarded my sincere appreciation for these things to be a gift. Back to school yet again facing the same problems I had left behind. How I wished I could get away from this terrible environment. On the first day one big bully, Pearman, got his willy stuck in an ink well, I cannot give an explanation to why it was there but the situation did create a huge laughing audience. Not amused by this disturbance the approaching master gave the whole class, the cane. God, how many days in a week do you see a kid with an ink well on the end of his willy? No sense of humour our master.

Jesus came into my life very early, he didn't stay very long but turned out to be a good guide, almost an invisible friend, I could trust. I had attended Sunday School enjoying the biblical stories but growing up gave me ideas that perhaps I should have kept to myself. The truth was I couldn't come to terms with the vicars of this world. The beautiful Virgin Mary gave birth to a great guy, err, okay but let's try this one. I got this idea from the Eagle comic. Spacemen came to planet Earth planting super human seeds (artificial insemination) trying to set an example to us all. It was Joseph that was the miracle, how he kept his hands off that beautiful Mary, God knows. Now you try to negotiate that with a vicar and all hells is let loose. I left the church that I had loved so dearly. Religion has been the cause of many problems in our world from pushing red-hot pokers up some poor sods undercarriage, dunking so called witches to bloody great wars. I'm not saying today's church is wrong but I have my own way of understanding Jesus. Civilisation should equal 100% human emotions like Jesus, we're about 2% with a long way to go, following Jesus will get us there, quicker.

The memory of my first flight, my endless passion for more flying was frustrating. To fly again I needed money and I had to get to Margate, impossible, my paper round funds would not meet the high cost of such a hobby and both Mum and Dad were not in the financial position to help.

Returning home from school one day I was informed by our neighbour that Mum and Dad had moved. Funny I thought, they never mentioned that to me. He bundled me into his car and delivered me to our new home. 2 Wendover Road, Well Hall, again South East London. We had moved from one very old council tip to an old newly painted one. The new home brought me closer to Kent. Using my old naval telescope I could see jets disappearing over the southern horizon. I identified the aircraft as R.A.F. Meteors. Dad told me that the aircraft were landing at the famous Battle of Britain base, Biggin Hill, about ten miles away. Knowing my enthusiasm for aviation he promised to take me to the Battle of Britain air show in September, but only if I was a good boy. Good boy, I was 18 carat gold for weeks, wondering how I could hold out until the big day.

I have included this photograph hoping that Ricky will contact me. He was great fun but I still do not understand his sudden disappearance. Another great pal was John Proctor from Eltham, South East London. Friends lost in time.

A coach party from a pub. Destination Margate 1952.

The coach would have departed from the Plumstead area, destined for Margate and to fulfil my dreams of flying. Little Ricky stands left behind the accordion player with me to the right. How we all wish to put the clock back when looking at photographs of our past. No chance, so forward.

Chapter 2

During the early 1950's Biggin Hill was a very beautiful area surrounded by undulating countryside. During that period I had the opportunity to cycle through the valley and was amazed at the unmade roads and tracks; each with a variety of dwellings almost hidden by the vast array of green foliage that was transformed into golden brilliance each Autumn. There I could be on my own, but never lonely, absorbing the beauty of my airfield and my England. Little was I to know that my life was about to change and bring me untold social wealth. Returning home with a rusty nose from the airport's wire fence was to be a thing of the past.

Joseph J. Merchant 1986

September 1952. The Battle of Britain Air Show at Royal Air Force Station, Biggin Hill, had arrived at long last. Dad and I caught the bus from Well Hall to Eltham, then a 126 red bus to Bromley and from there the 410 Green country bus took us to Biggin Hill via Keston Ponds and Chicken Farm Bend. The traffic in those days was bad and it took us more than 2 hours to complete the journey. Entering R.A.F. Biggin Hill through the main gate took us to the very strange road system of the West Camp that led us to the static display area. The thousands of people there initially made me feel insignificant, but, the sight of the R.A.F. aircraft soon made me feel at home. There were Meteors by the score. R.A.F. Biggin Hill had the three squadrons of this aircraft type at that time. N° 41 Squadron Royal Air Force and two Royal Auxiliary Air Force Squadrons, 600 and 615. I drooled at sight of so many different aircraft, tugging on my Dad's sleeve not to miss a thing. The weather was just right for the event, warm with blue skies. The R.A.F. had parked a Meteor on the firing range and for an unknown sum of money, that Dad paid, you got the chance to fire the guns and have your photo taken by one of the ground crew. The are two reasons I have included this picture below; (i) It was my first visit to R.A.F. Biggin Hill. (ii) I wonder how many other boys fired those guns on that very special day.

As recorded by British Pathe News

My first visit to R.A.F. Biggin Hill September 1952

Can you imagine Health and Safety allowing such activity today, no chance. Returning home with memories of the R.A.F. "At Home" at Biggin Hill, I would now have to wait 364 days until the next visit to this historic airfield. Happy, you couldn't buy that feeling. Sold out!

Young boy's treasure.

This programme from 1952 gave me endless pleasure knowing that I would, one day, return to R.A.F. Biggin Hill. The winter ahead was not the ideal time to stand at the end of the runway. I can only remember cycling once to Biggin during this period with little flying from the Royal Air Force.

Once I knew the route to Biggin Hill I was back there, by bus or bike whenever possible. However, the long cold winters limited my visits, for there was no welcome at the main gate nor shelter from the rain. I took the opportunity to start collecting Kellogg's aviation cards, books and the odd aircraft magazine. My friends used to call me "Jet Joe", corny maybe but the sight of any aircraft gave me so much pleasure. I ate, slept and drank aviation. On reflection it was a very lonely existence, purely because I had no one with whom to share my enthusiasm with. My Sister Jean was already married and Rosemary heading in the same direction. Mum and Dad came from a very different world to the one I was yearning for. During the summer months of 1953 my visits to R.A.F. Biggin Hill became my week-end pastime; pushing my nose through that wire fencing, waiting for the appearance of my favourite Meteor, see drawing below. I had little knowledge of squadron numbers and markings at this time due to the many restrictions in place during the cold war era.

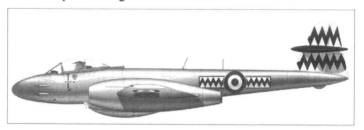

Copyright Clavework Graphics

615 Sqn. R.Aux.A.F. Squadron Leader's Aircraft

At last I met another aviation freak who has since turned out to be one of my lifelong friends, his name Alan Hogg. At last things seem to be improving. Now we could discuss the latest machines without having the Mickey taken out of us. Can you imagine what my life would have been if I had been a knitting enthusiast. These were exciting times when Britain was producing some of the best aircraft in the world. The Hawker Hunter flown by Neville Duke. The Vickers Supermarine Swift, the de Havilland 110 and many others. Alan and I spent many happy hours talking about aviation and riding our bikes to R.A.F. Biggin Hill. Alan came from a military family with one of his sisters, June, an officer in the girls organisation called the Women's Junior Air Corps. Later this was renamed The Girls Venture Corps sharing headquarters with the local Air Training Corps Squadron. BINGO! - FREE FLYING was in sight.

Chapter Two

May 4th 1954 without doubt another turning point in my young life. Along with Alan Hogg I attended the Friday evening parade of 56(F) Squadron, Air Training Corps, at Wellington Street, Woolwich, South East London. Immediately I was at home, loving the bull and brass that all the young lads were put through.

"Stand up when I'm talking to you." Yelled the Sergeant.
You have to look around to see who's lying down.

"You 'orrible little man" was another favourite little gem they used when making reference to the cadets. You either took it as it was, or you joined a more civilised youth organisation away from the pre-military service training. Fortunately I had never been happier at the thought of free clothing, food and flying. Every day was Christmas day. The squadron's basic training was brilliant. The cadets came in all shapes and sizes, were from different backgrounds, but were brought together into a cohesive unit by the strict discipline applied by the Officers and NCO's (Non Commissioned Officers). It would be the first time in my life I understood the true meaning of comradeship, we marched, ate and even went to the loo together. Our basic training was split into two categories. The parade ground and the class room. We studied Theory of Flight, Morse Code, Map Reading, Engines and Aircraft Recognition. The parade ground activities were to see whether you could destroy all your brains cells in less than one hour, they included marching, foot drill, rifle drill and the Squadron Band. This was the pinnacle of success.

The three months probation period seemed like a lifetime but the great day eventually arrived and I was ordered to the Commanding Officer's Office for my acceptance interview. Flight Lieutenant "Tug" Wilson, our Commanding Officer, interviewed all the boys before the issue of their uniforms and R.A.F. Form 3822. This small booklet was the key to all happiness; it included your parent's authorisation for all the activities you would take part in at summer camps; such as 303 Rifle range practice and flying. Flying, but when, how long would I have to wait for some action in the blue. After a short chat with "Tug" I was off to the stores to collect my uniform. I had already purchased my boots having saved money from my paper-round. I was ready to do all the damage to my brain cells the Sergeant's demanded of me. *"Left right, left right, look up, look up"* screamed the Sergeant. I joined this lot to look down, not up. Everything seemed to be carried out by numbers "And Oner and twoer". The issue of equipment was a new experience. Rifles one, rounds six, the same as belts one, gaiters two, cross-belt one, it was all back to front. To this day I can say I never found out, why. Boots black was another example. Flying nil. I was getting somewhat worried my life was flying by leaving me on the ground. I was now 14 years and 3 months and yet to be an ace. Warrant Officer "Ernie"Gauge's main objective seemed to centre on the destruction of the parade ground. After only one week in uniform the squadrons notice board attracted my attention. "R.Aux.A.F. attachment at Biggin Hill" I removed this priceless document from the notice board ran upstairs to "Tug's" office, panting like a Jack Russell on heat. I knocked firmly on the CO's door.

"Come in." Came the firm and familiar voice of Flight Lieutenant Taylor, our Squadron Adjutant,

"Ah young Merchant what can be done for you." He asked.

I thrust the notice onto the CO's desk requesting permission to attend Biggin Hill for the next two week-ends.

"Sorry Merchant you're the only cadet that has made application and we understand the minimum number is four cadets." He replied.

My concern was like a boiling kettle, it's already Friday evening, final parade is in 10 minutes.

"Sir, with permission I have the other cadets downstairs talking to Sergeant Prigon, should I fetch them?" I said biting my lying tongue.

"As it's almost time for final parade give me the names then." Said Tug.

I saluted, left the lying den as quickly as possible, rushed downstairs and grabbed Alan Hogg, Johnny Bevan and Ron Fairhurst saying.

"We're off to Biggin Hill for two week-ends starting tomorrow can you all make it."

"To bloody true." Said Ron.

"Count me in." Replied Alan, while Johnny nodded. I took that as a yes.

"Final parade in 5, when Tug asks for the Biggin Hill Attachment names give yours loud and clear." I ordered.

Twenty minutes later I held in my hand a document of authority to attend at R.A.F. Biggin Hill the following morning. Arrangements were made for us to meet at the 126 bus stop in Eltham. Returning home that evening and telling Mum & Dad what was going to happen to me made little or no difference to their coming weekend. I went into the back garden to see if Margaret, one of our neighbours, was around. I had to tell somebody; no, I had to tell the world. The truth was, however, that only Alan, Ron and Johnny shared the same enthusiasm. I looked up to the clear sky, stars, millions of stars, happy thinking. *"Should I ever go up there, Mum would have to pack lot's of sandwiches in my lunch tin."*

We had little idea what the cadet attachment duties were or to whom, we had to report. I understood the Royal Auxiliary Air Force. They were also known as weekend boys as apposed to the Brylcreem boys, i.e., full time R.A.F. Officers. We didn't really give any thought to what the week-end's adventure might bring. It was, after all Biggin Hill, and what more could any human want? I had spent the last two years cycling up to Biggin Hill pushing my nose through that wire fence, now I would be on the inside looking out. Then came the thoughts of polishing the squadron transport, sweeping out dirty buildings, perhaps the only jets we might see would be old discarded photos. WRONG! The following photographs exemplifies the activities to be seen during the "nose through the fence" period, 52/53 at R.A.F. Biggin Hill.

615 Squadron R.Aux.A.F. Cold War exercise. 6th April 1952

This badly damaged image was found in an old air show programme and is unique inasmuch it shows 615 Squadron Meteors Mk 8's operating from the South Camp while awaiting completion of the South East apron and a new hangar. Before delivery of the Mk.T7 Meteor (Trainer) during 1953 the Squadron was issued with North American Harvard's (Also visible in this picture.). From my limited aviation knowledge, I must say having the Harvard as a check out aircraft for the Meteor was, or must have been exciting to say the least. The propeller driven Harvard with tail wheel, versus the twin-jet Meteor with a nose wheel, provided a very different experience for the pilots. The T11 Vampire would have made life a lot longer. I think the M.o.D. should have had a surplus of this aircraft during the early 50's judging from the deliveries of Vampires, of which there were many going both to the R.A.F. and overseas customers.

The pilots used leather type flying helmets notwithstanding the fact that the Meteor Mk 8 was fitted with a Martin Baker ejection seat. Later in this book I shall describe, in great detail, the introduction of the Bone-Dome (Hard-Hat) to our weekend flyers.

Photos: Via Dan Graham

615 Squadron Royal Auxiliary Air Force Biggin Hill 1952

Meteor Mk 8 all silver finish with the old type canopy. The boss during these years was a Sqn. Ldr. Sowrey who took over the unit from Sqn. Ldr. N. Duke. Sqn. Ldr. "Bob" Eeles took command during 1953.

WF 639 refuelling on the South Camp. WF 684 in the background.

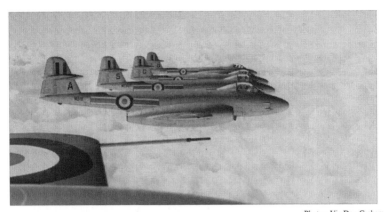

Photos: Via Dan Graham

41 Squadron R.A.F. Biggin Hill 1952.
Gloster Meteor's Mk .8's WB111 - WE867 - WE943 - WA962

41 Squadron, the last operational fighter squadron, took delivery of their Meteors during 1951. By 1955 the squadron was operating Hawker Hunters which were to be the last fighter type to operate from R.A.F. Biggin Hill.

1953

R.A.F. Biggin Hill wing preparing for take off for the Coronation fly past. Only one noise complaint and that came from the F.O. Pilot at the back.

11th September 1953 I witnessed a large formation of Meteors through my school windows flying between 1,000 and 1,500 feet, suddenly one aircraft appeared to pull up into the inverted position disappearing out of my view. Later that day I was to learn that two of the aircraft had collided , one coming down in the danger building area of the Royal Arsenal at Woolwich. It narrowly missed two buildings containing high explosives.

The pilot, Wing Commander Robert Duncan Yule D.F.C. - D.S.O. lost his life. The other aircraft involved, piloted by Yule's number two, sustained a shattered cockpit canopy inflicting temporary concussion on the pilot. Escorted by yet another of the Meteors he was able to land his damaged aircraft at R.A.F. North Weald. To my knowledge both aircraft came from 245 Squadron based at R.A.F. Horsham St. Faith. The Evening Standard was onto this story rapidly launching a helicopter to get a few air to ground photographs of the wreckage and local damage. This they did but suffered a very heavy fine of £10,000 for flying over a restricted area and endangering life by flying too close to National Grid power lines. Silly Billie's.

Photo: Via Dan Graham

St. George's Chapel of Remembrance

St George's Chapel was completed in 1951. This photograph was taken after the arrival of both gate guardians during 1954. Left - Spitfire LF MkXVle SL674. Right - Hurricane IIcb LF738

Chapter 3

Life's riches are not measured in wealth alone, they come in many ways. As a young boy I was happy and contented among my friends. A child's life is a somewhat regimented environment and doesn't necessarily alert one to the responsibilities to be confronted later. I was like a starving animal unable to control the urgent need to feed, but my hunger was for the happiness of a rich dream come true. As for the responsibilities they became part of the happiness that I carried with pride. Why, though, did we laugh so much?.

Joseph J. Merchant 1987

As planned all four cadets met in Eltham catching the 126 bus to Bromley and then the 410 to Biggin Hill. Our journey was one of excited chat, what would we see and who would we meet? The 410 bus stop was almost outside the main gate. On arrival we approached the main guard room smartly. This appeared to be a breeding ground for Service Police. God how many police do you need to cover an airfield, my aside to Alan did not improve the atmosphere either,

"Don't step out of line here Alan or trouble will be your surname."

I had learnt the nickname for these chaps during my first days with the ATC, they were known as."Rock Apes." Now, not having had any social time with apes I had little idea of its meaning. They were extremely smart in their blue uniforms with white blancoed webbing, but lacked the air of overall authority, very strange.

"Good morning Sergeant."

I said, handing him the authorisation slip stating our reason for being alive.

"We are four cadets from 56 Squadron reporting for attachment duties with the Royal Auxiliary Air Force, Sergeant."

I immediately sensed that his Mother-in-Law must be staying for the weekend. He was far from happy making unusual noises, grunting and puffing away. He rotated the signing-in sheet and grunted.

"Sign en."

All four of us complied, not saying a word apart from Alan whispering

"I can't see who's pulling the strings."

Thus implying our sergeant was being controlled by some another means. Oh, was I in pain trying so hard not to laugh. Signing in completed, our sergeant reached through a cut out window into the office and produced a map of the airfield giving instructions in his broad East London accent..

"Right, yar foller the outta road 'til yer reach an 'angar, yer knows wot an 'angar is don't cher? It's like a garidge only big. Keep ta the right of the hairfield and when yar cross the end of the runway look boff ways to make sure it an't in use. The traffic lights are for cars, not 'umans. If yar get half way across and you idenhify an heroplane takin hoff, then run like mad. Carry on 'til you see anoffer 'angar and report to the duty Sergeant"

"How long should this take us Sergeant?" I asked.

"About an 'our, now off yer go."

His duty was completed, so he thought.

"Sergeant." I said. "Would it be possible for MT (Motor Transport) to provide us with a Land Rover to save us...?"

I said no more.

He started to change colour, veins protruding from his broad neck and there followed the most amazing high volume command:

"Git your arse out of 'ere, what do yar fink this is a bleeding taxi rank."
We departed trying to control our laughter at this highly excitable NCO. We marched through West Camp keeping to the outer road of the airfield until we reached the first hangar. There were a few Meteors parked casually outside bringing our mounting excitement to an almost dangerous level. Each one of us desperately trying to beat the other at spotting something new. The next sighting made my stomach pull around 3 G's. A Meteor with blue zigzags running down the fuselage and taxiing towards us. We stopped, throwing the pilot a salute and he responded with a wave. Bloody hell, no bloody marvellous. We passed the end of the runway safely then two Meteors took off.

"Bloody noisy." Alan shouted.
"Paradise, absolutely sheer paradise." I replied.
We continued our march towards the second hangar, as instructed by our sweet Sergeant. There we were greeted by a line of Meteors, all with blue zigzags painted on their fuselages. However, the first aircraft also had those same zigzags on the fin and rudder. It was the very Meteor I had waited to see on so many of my visits to Biggin Hill. Now, there it was. I was stunned by this dream come true thinking. *"What was I doing here, why was this happening to me?"* It was as if all sound, light and motion had been frozen. The sudden shout from a Sergeant would bring me back to earth very quickly.

"Right lads report to the NCO's office right away."

The excitement was increasing with the squadron now going into action, pilots were climbing into the aircraft and ground crews running in all directions. The noise, the smell, it was heaven, but it was also very difficult to concentrate on what was being said to us. Arriving at the N.C.O's office we were each given a set of R.A.F. overalls, God, as if we weren't hot enough already. I Removed my dog collar tunic, which was then standard issue, climbed into the smelly garment hoping I would not receive a telling off since I had on both a R.A.F. blue shirt and a black tie. These were not permitted for cadets but nothing was said and we continued being intro-duced to the sergeants who were to be responsible for our training.

Ground safety was the first lecture. This involved the moving of aircraft with the aid of a Land Rover or alternatively with the help of many 'erks.'

Collision with hangar doors would appear to be a big problem. Repairs to a Meteors wing due to kissing a hangar door £350.00, so we were taught 'slowly doe's it.' Always 'erks' on each point of the aircraft. Parking aircraft inside a hangar produced the same problem, commonly known as 'hanger rash.' Other subjects taught to us were, aircraft covers, ejection seats, and do not go near the cockpit without authorisation. The latter that was a very quick lecture. Aircraft chocks, in a hangar. Yes, I found it hard to believe that you would chock an aircraft inside hangar. This was our first and valuable lesson working with aircraft. As an A.T.C. Cadet, yet to take any exams for promotion, I was known as Cadet Merchant AC 2. Now to give you a true perspective of this rank I should say that a snake's arse is higher in respect-ability than the AC2. I was promoted to 'erk' on my first day, bloody marvellous I was now cleared to move large pieces of aluminium on wheels from A to B; an ERK.' Tea break, that's when we were introduced to the rest of the squadron's ground crews, the other 'erks'. All I wanted to do was to get to my favourite Meteor but there were more lectures to come.

Tea break over we assembled outside with our Sergeant,
"Right, refuelling the Meteor, follow me." He said.
I'm sure you could have put a complete Mars Bar, in Alan's mouth, side-ways. Nothing was said and we followed our leader towards the line of aircraft. Getting closer the whole squadron looked brand new, not the silver finish I had expected but camouflaged top side with dull silver underside. The initial shock of seeing the blue zigzag marking had distracted my overall vision of the aircraft's colour scheme. The Sergeant turned saying.
"Right, the Meteor Mk. 8 has 2 fixed fuel tanks. These are called the main tanks, also known as top tanks and there is also a belly tank,"
"Now check the lads on the belly." He ordered a Corporal.
The Corporal took us around the aircraft to a parked fuel bowser. One by one we were given instructions on applying the fuel line to the belly tank and finally the top tanks. Within 30 minutes all four cadets had been checked out on refuelling the Meteor Mk. 8. By now it was mid-day, in the middle of August, it was warm, and very quiet. All the aircraft had returned, been refuelled and ready to go again. Then a shout from the NCO'S office announced
"Lunch coach in five minutes."
All the 'erks' and NCO'S removed their overalls and proceeded towards the west end of the hangar. We followed not knowing what to expect. Sure enough one R.A.F. Blue coach arrived and off we all went to experience the

airmen's mess menu. Now I like to think its best to say things about people, in all walks of life, but who ever prepared that meal should have been taken away placed in a food mixer and flushed down a drain, the taste resembled an oil change on Dad's Austin Van, and the baked potatoes were the answer to the M.o.D. if ever it ran out of ammunition. Hard, you couldn't cut them you had to break them. Having made the best of our free meal it was time to catch the coach back to our squadron, yes our very own squadron, 615 Royal Auxiliary Air Force, Biggin Hill. I'm not sure how many aircraft we refuelled that afternoon but I can say we were always under the eagle eyes of our faithful Corporals, and 'erks' who took pride in giving us the opportunity to live in this man's world. We all loved it, smelly, dirty and hungry. Tea up, yet another life saving Mars Bar, I lost track of time, too engrossed to be thinking of returning home. That feeling of loss and emptiness came back, but this time I thought I'm not going to lose this and we'll be back tomorrow. It was time to put all the Meteors away for the night. A lot of people wouldn't understand, but placing my dirty hands on an aircraft gave me a feeling of;

"Christ this is heavy." I cried to my Sergeant.

"Push, push." Was the only sympathy I got in return.

All eight fighters had to be moved into the hanger, four each side, and the Mk.T7 trainer in the centre, ready for doors open tomorrow. Again a voice from the NCO's office.

"Coach to R.A.F. Kidbrook in 30 minutes."

R.A.F. Kidbrook, that's 20 minutes walk from my home, same as Ron's. Alan and Johnny would have to catch a bus at Well Hall to their destinations. First day was over, free food, free clothing, albeit smelly, free tuition and now free transport. I must meet up with that Sergeant S.P. and tell him the M.T. section's vehicles are satisfactory for our requirements. That should wind him up. The chat on our journey home was wonderful we relived the moments of this incredible day. I was exhausted with joy seeing and touching my favourite Meteor. I had learnt that this aircraft was the boss's, a Squadron Leader "Bob" Eeles. My next objective was to meet him.

On arrival home Mum and Dad had gone out, I rushed to the back garden to see if Margaret was around. I had to bore the pants off somebody and none better than my Margaret.. We were great friends usually spending summer time together but now she would have to take second place to Biggin Hill. Not that it ever affected our youth.

Sunday morning and we are back at the Biggin Hill Guardroom and who was the duty Sergeant? You guessed it, our lovely, friendly, helpful Rock Ape.

"Good morning Sergeant, what a beautiful day." I said.

"Is that a remark or a question." He replied.

Turning the signing-in sheet for our attention he sarcastically asked.

"Enjoy your little walk yesterday then err?".

"We had the opportunity to have the use of a R.A.F. coach yesterday and we would like to thank the M. T. section, most satisfactory. Would you be so kind to pass that message of thanks on Sergeant?..."

Again it was prudent to say no more in view of the Sergeants reaction. We left the Guardroom at speed. Now just around the corner from the guard room was the M. T. section, free transport. I knocked on the door calling for attention when a Corporal said

"Good morning, can we help?"

"Four cadets needing to report to Sqn. Ldr. Eeles, 615 Squadron, at 9.30 hours. Can you help?"

His reaction pleased me ordering an 'erk to deliver us to 615 and seven minutes later we were on the south east apron at our squadron. It was the manner of the request that got results, but I wondered JUST how many times it would work. The Sunday took on a similar pattern as Saturday, the weather was beautiful with the squadron taking full advantage of the clear skies, spirits were running high with both air and ground crews enjoying this atmosphere of all is well. Tea breaks, lunch time, and getting to know more of the 'erks', great bunch of happy chappies always ready to give one help and advice on the squadron's activities. After such a short time I felt part of this brilliant unit and on this day I would have the opportunity to talk to some of the aircrew. I had learnt not to ask silly question, like.

"Do you like flying Sir".

No, my approach was.

"Sir, I wonder if you could spare me a moment as I feel I have upset a Military Policeman and most concerned of the out come."

Well there was a possibility that our Three striped Ape might pay the squadron a visit looking for me.

"You didn't hit him did you?" Asked one of the crew.

" No Sir, not on this occasion."

I replied which appeared to create a giggle.

"What on earth have you done to concern yourself with such a matter."

Asked another member of the group. I related the saga of both mornings encounters of the transport request and my suggestion that the Sergeant pass on our sincere thanks to MT, when we were asked to leave the guardroom in no polite terms. The group burst into laughter with a comments from one of the crew

"Damn long walk from the guardroom to the squadron."

"No Sir, not this morning, we got a lift in a Land Rover from M. T."

The laughter became louder with one officer assuring me I had no problem. I felt honoured to have had this small window of opportunity to share some time with the aircrew suddenly realising the officer slightly behind me listening to my story was a Squadron Leader. Jesus, it was the boss. Who's first and only comment was.

"I take it the new batch of cadets are being looked after and all is well."

"Yes, thank you Sir." I replied nervously.

I wanted to continue the conversation but I had two thousand words stuck in my throat unable to dislodge them. I eventually thanked the group of officers for their time and returned to my duties.

Finishing our tea break a Sergeant poked his head round the canteen door saying.

"Hogg, Fairhurst, Merchant, Bevan, report to the armoury."

I didn't know we had one. Finding this double size room we were given instruction on the cleaning of 20 mm cannon shells after aircraft completed a live firing exercise. Each aircraft had a different colour applied to the shells so in the event of a pilot hitting a towed target his success could be seen by the colour left on the target. On landing an armourer would unload remaining shells from each aircraft and deliver them to 'erks' like us to clean, ready for repainting on the next sortie. The method for cleaning was a basin of solvent and a brush. Not pleasant, but when the job was finished you felt you had helped the squadron complete its mission and hoping the chaps wouldn't go playing cowboys the following weekend. Then the now familiar voice.

"R.A.F. Kidbrook coach in 30 minutes."

Tired, dirty, smelly. but I was so happy with the achievements of our week-end. The following days dragged by so very slowly. At last the Friday parade, the other cadets couldn't believe our stories of our first week-end with the Auxiliaries. Even our senior NCO., W. O. Gage was pleased to listen of our adventure. Final parade, home, bed and back to Biggin Hill tomorrow knowing that we had a whole week-end of excitement ahead no matter what duty one was allocated nor how dirty it might be.

Back to Biggin Hill and again the weather was good to us, warm with cumulus clouds. We no longer had to worry about our Ape at the guardroom as our ground crews friends told us of a quick way to the squadron. The 410 bus took us past the main R.A.F. entrance and on to the Village Green bus stop. From there we walked back to a small road next to the Nightingale Café (Now Squires Timber) ten minutes later we were in our smelly's ready for the day's duties. Refuelling the aircraft as they returned from their exercises was so very easy, but always under the eagle eyes of our faithful seniors. I was on belly tanks with Ron; Alan for some unknown reason volunteered to fill the wing tanks. We had not been checked out on this small container that improved the look of the Meteor but was very unusual to see on a 615's aircraft. I had just completed my first belly when I saw Alan receive a face full of Avtag. He had not been looking into the tank to check the fuel level, the only way to see if it was full. Two chaps grabbed Alan, another took the bowser hose from him, they rushed him to the gents toilet and applied vast amounts of water to his eyes. Alan was temporarily blinded and in some discomfort from his unfortunate experience. By lunch time his sight had returned though still in pain he continued to apply water to his eyes as instructed by our Sergeant.

We all returned from lunch around 13.30 hours only to witness the most amazing scene. Pilots had started to receive their new flying helmets (Bone Domes) to replace the 1946 vintage brown leather type. The chatter was quite intense with views coming from each and every pilot on the pros and cons of this new equipment.

"The interior is fine but the egg shell I don't like." said one of the crew.

"You need that for protection just in case you have to go through the canopy." said another.

"It's far too heavy and it makes me look like a motorcyclist." said an outsider. Then a senior officer made it very clear that the equipment had been tested and passed by the R.A.F. Flight Safety people.

"I can't turn my head round wearing that bloody thing." said one chap.

"The only thing that turns your head around is that blonde WAAF in the control tower and boy do you need some controlling." reported his friend. The group was increasing in numbers due to the laughter, pilots seem to arrive from every door in the building, all joining in on the discussion. The comments came thick and fast

"No it doesn't."

"Yes it will, I read it in Flight Safety"

"Have you used one yet?"

"My Dad didn't."

The laughter became infectious with both aircrews and ground staff enjoying the banter. The senior officer then declared there was only one answer. a test needed by our own squadron to prove its effectiveness.

Illustration by Arthur Benjamin 2011

The test as carried out by 615 Sqn. R.Aux.A.F. Biggin Hill 1954

The pronounced thud as the Air Ministry Works Department brick hit the helmet was a worrying moment. Quickly followed by the pilot standing, unharmed, to the clapping and cheers of all the crews. Test completed! Back to operations. Before we knew it came.

"Kidbrook coach in 30 minutes."

That call I didn't want to hear.

Sunday, our last day. I could say that the duties had became boring, but the fact that one was a part of the team tasked with ensuring the squadron was kept at operational readiness made it a real challenge. We were encouraged to do our best always. There were magic moments of fun and banter with the ground crews. Get cheeky though, and you were in trouble. On one occasion I over stepped my position and ended with my head down the toilet followed by the royal flush. On another occasion, after we had put the aircraft away, I was locked in the T7. Hanger doors closed, lights out, bloody dark. However 15 minutes later a Sergeant opened the canopy and said.

" Who's been a cheeky lad then. Off you go, you don't want to miss your coach."

It was scary in that cockpit. I was well aware the aircraft was not fitted with an ejector seat, so I didn't have that worry, but the thought of spending the night there was frightening.

Having the opportunity to spend more time with the aircrew we were invited to see the cine film results of the previous weeks live shoot. This was another real treat for us, to actually seeing what the pilots got up to once they had left Biggin Hill. No sound on the film just the results of each pilot's efforts to hit a towed target. The small room was full of pilots, plus a few Sergeants who remained silent throughout the whole event.

"That's you Tony I'm sure." Said a voice from the dark.

"How do you know it was my shoot?" Asked his friend.

"Must be yours, you missed the bloody target."

Then a voice of some authority named the pilots 1 to 4. Going through the film again the officer took a grip on this meeting.

"Number One. Missed." Big boo from the audience.

"Number two. A full hit." Big cheer went up.

"Number three. A full hit." Louder cheer.

"Number four. Missed." Bigger boo.

Then one of the team told the story of the Australian tug pilots comments to the four ship leader.

"Tell that number four of yours I'm pulling this f+++++g thing not pushing it."

The roar of laughter ended the meeting. I remember our big Sergeant wiping the tears from his eyes, his large body heaving with uncontrolled laughter. As the room cleared we had the chance to thank the senior officer for our invitation and he commented on the results as.

"Not a good show, perhaps better next time. Good to see you." Strange I thought, here was an officer saying that to 14 year old cadets. I was learn-ing

these officers were special people, well educated, extremely polite and considerate to others, even young ATC cadets.

The weekend was coming to a close and it seemed that my dream was about to end. Talking with my friends, Alan, Ron and seemed that our only option was to apply for an extension through our own ATC squadron. But there were still things to be done for the afternoon was very active. Time seemed to evaporate with so many aircraft movements. I don't know why but we had to collect one of our Meteors from 600 Squadron, on the North East side of Biggin. We all jumped in the squadron's Land Rover, and were off to 600. Tow bar attached to the nose wheel we returned very slowly to 615 with Alan on one wing me on the other. Time to think again, I didn't want to lose this wonderful life, these special people and of course the aircraft. It all meant so much to me. The Sergeants were great treating us like men. The time came to say goodbye to Sqn. Ldr. "Bob Eeles." However this was not to be. He announced,

"You are to be my personal guests, and attend the squadron as you please."
"Thank you sir." Saluting my rapid departure.

The following weekend, Sunday the 5th September, the Squadron Honorary Air Commodore, Sir Winston Churchill, was due to present the boss with the Esher Trophy. We had already been informed by our Sergeants that the following weekend was a clean up and practice for the cadets, not that we were due to attend the squadron as we had completed our two week period. Back at 56 ATC Woolwich it was not advisable to mention the open invitation of 615 to turn up as, and when we wished, was not the way things worked.

615 Squadron R.Aux.A.F. was awarded the Esher Trophy for efficiency in 1953. With the permission from Flight Magazine I reproduce below their report on the presentation of that award by Sir Winston Churchill, the then Prime Minister and Honorary Air Commodore of 615 Squadron.

"Undoubtedly to his own satisfaction and to that of every member of the Squadron, Sir Winston Churchill presented the trophy to 615 Squadron R.Aux.A.F. of which he has been the Honorary Air Commodore for the last 15 years. Addressing the squadron, the then Prime Minister recalled the origins of the Auxiliary Squadrons, praising their members for giving up week-ends and holidays to help maintain Britain's fame and prowess in the

*air. "The achievement we celebrate today," he said, "would never have
been won if both officers and airmen of 615 Squadron had not given very
much more of their time and attendance than the legal minimum required.
Much credit falls to Sqn. Ldr. Sowrey, who was in command during the
whole of 1953 and to Sqn. Ldr. Eeles, who has now succeeded him." He then
thanked Sqn.Ldr. Neville Duke, who commanded the squadron during the
running-up period last year when the squadron came second. After the
ceremony, while taking tea in the officers mess, Sir Winston beckoned to
Sqn. Ldr. Cormack of 600 Squadron- the mortal "enemies"of 615 at Biggin
Hill-and dictated to him a telegram he wished sent to H. M. Queen Elizabeth
the Queen Mother, who was the Honorary Air Commodore of 600. It read:
600 Squadron in their humble duty convey the respects of the Prime
Minister, who has today presented the Esher Trophy to his squadron."*

Flight photo

Sqn. Ldr "Bob" Eeles receiving the Esher Trophy from Sir Winston. South East Apron 1954.

This presentation must have been Bob's proudest moment during his command of 615 knowing he was following in the footsteps of previous squadron commanders whose efforts had made this achievement possible.

AC 2 Ron Fairhurst. Wearing the smelly's

This Image was taken on the South East apron, 615 Squadron H.Q. almost the same spot where Churchill had presented the Easher Trophy to Sqn. Ldr. "Bob" Eeles. West Camp can be seen in the background, the H.Q. Of 41 Squadron. This Meteor Mk.8 WK648 was converted to a U-16 Drone during 1961 and then written off on 1st October 1963. Shame!

Being accepted and encouraged by my superiors gave me confidence within this mans world. Working with and among my hero's gave me a true perspective of their value, understanding the price paid by their many colleagues in darker days. The old soldier became my idol.

Chapter Three

Chapter 4

The loud bang as the hangar doors closed signified the end of another weekend of flying. The only time, I felt the tingle of the goose pimples run through my body was the closure of the day. R.A.F. Biggin Hill, its people and aircraft was now the most important part of my young life and was helping me overcome the loss of a dearest friend due to her parents moving their home. Later a greater pain would be thrust upon me leaving only memories of the Royal Auxiliary Air Force, a unique and irreplaceable period.

Joseph J. Merchant 1989

Johnny Bevan went missing he had left the cadets, never to be seen again. Alan never returned to Biggin Hill, so it was Ron and I that would break all the rules. I was a little worried that we would be found out attending 615 without the permission of our Commanding Officer. The winter proved hard, both in work and weather, we soon learned you needed old newspaper under your pyjamas that were under your uniform that was under the overalls issued by the squadron. Cold , Biggin Hill is 600 feet above sea level and when there's a North East wind, it's bitterly cold laying on cold tarmac refuelling Meteor belly tanks, painful, but we did it.

My first flight with the ATC was from Biggin Hill to Kenley in a Avro Anson. I had little idea so much string was used by the R.A.F. This aircraft was obviously getting ready for a posting to the scrap yard. My second flight was in a Chipmunk at our 1955 summer camp at R.A.F. Duxford. It was the last flight of the day and permission was given for us to do aerobatics over the airfield, my first time being upside down. Wonderful. I remember seeing the two squadrons of Meteors lined up on the large Duxford apron. Numbers 64 and 65 were based at Duxford during that period.

Summer and life at Biggin became more comfortable. In August 1955 when we had been attending the squadron for almost a year Bob, our boss, said
  "It's time to get you some experience in the Meteor. "
Again it was the Mars bar in the mouth sideways plus another two thousand words lodged in our throats. Ron and I looked at each other.
  "When Sir? " We both asked
  "Next weekend, is that okay with you both, no other duties? " He asked.
  "No sir, that's super. " I replied.
However it could create problems. The allocation of cadets for attachment to R.Aux.A.F. Squadrons, flying and overseas camps was carried out by senior reserve officers within the ATC. We were definitely jumping the queue without permission. On one occasion at 615 I was pulled up by a ATC Inspection Warrant Officer who asked me which squadron I was with. How the hell he knew I was a ATC cadet, damn it was my beret. My R.A.F. blue shirt and black tie did the job but the beret tucked in my trousers let the cat out of the bag. The ATC badge is silver, the R.A.F. gold.
  "Good morning W.O. I'm from 56 Squadron special attachment under the command of Sdn. Lrd Eeles. Do you need to talk to him? " I replied .

"Oh, oh no. I had been informed that Dulwich was the only squadron working here this weekend."He replied."

"Special duties W.O. I'm very surprised you were not informed of our special duties." Was my final remark as he waddled off tutting.

The excitement of Bob's suggestion that we should fly in the T7 over shadowed our real problem. We had no permission from our ATC H.Q.

"We do have a big problem Ron, not a word to the other lads until we have the flight in our log book." I said.

Both of us knew what we were doing was very wrong. The week at school was as bad as ever, long, dull. Friday evening, nothing was said at 56. Saturday we did not attend 615. Sunday 4th September 1955 back to the Biggin Hill full of enthusiasm for our day ahead. Although cameras were not permitted on R.A.F. Biggin Hill during this cold war period I could not resist taking my 120 box camera to record this special event. We reported to our boss on our arrival and were issued with head sets and allocated our pilots. I would fly first with Flying Officer Ian Smith. Ron would follow with Flight Lieutenant Pee Wee Judge. Little was said during the whole exercise of preparation , a mix of nerves, excitement and concern. For sure there would be a problem if we were to meet up with another ATC inspection officer. I could imagine Bob telling anyone that interfered with the workings of his squadron to bugger off but, both Ron and myself would be in big trouble back at 56. Ian Smith, my pilot, was a tall slim gentleman.

"Cadet Merchant." He said.

"Sir." I replied. *"We'll be off then, all ready?"* He said.

"Yes sir very much."

Walking across the grass towards the waiting Meteor Ian asked my flying experience.

"15 minutes joy flight at Margate. Biggin Hill to Kenley return in the Anson and 30 minutes aero's in the Chipmunk, Sir." I said proudly.

"Ah, the Chipmunk. One of my favourite aircraft. You enjoyed that?" He asked.

"Yes very much, my real first experience of G forces, finding the first manoeuvre a little strange. Will we experience G today sir?" I asked. Thinking those two thousand words that I had lodged in my throat had suddenly found an exit. I couldn't stop talking, asking endless questions on our trip. Ian had the most charming smile and seem to understand my excitement.

"Come on, let's go flying." He said.

Stepping up to the aircraft I was met by some of my erk friends who said nothing but.

"Jump in." As if it was a merry-go-round ride.

An erk fitted me into my parachute and seat harness that was very bulky and uncomfortable. Head set on, canopy closed, engines started. Ian asked me if I was ready to go which I replied

"Yes sir."

The aircraft moved slowly forward then stopped, brake test completed. I was learning. Then the engines wound up giving us the power to taxi clear of the apron. We crossed 29/11 runway heading for the East side of the airfield disturbing the many resident Lapwings that congregated in the long unattended grass areas. We came to a halt, then Ian ran both engines to full power. Jesus the noise, thinking. *"I bet that upset the Lapwings we had just passed."* We continued taxiing to runway 21 swinging into a southerly direction, then with full power on I was to experience G forces on take off. Half way down the runway the Meteor lifted off the runway and over the main road. Was there a little boy down there poking his nose through the fence watching me go flying. In a few seconds we reached 3000 feet levelled off flying around South East London. My school, I could see the bump plus Shrewsbury Park. If only I had a few bombs on board, problem over. We said very little during the flight due to my headset going intermittent. Reaching the Thames Ian turned the aircraft South, the concrete colour turning to green as we were now over Surrey and upside down. I caught a glimpse of an airport and that was one hell of a slow roll. Things were happening so fast, we were already back at R.A.F. Biggin Hill our flight was over. Taxiing back to the Squadron gave me a very different view of the South East apron with our Meteors lined up ready for flight.

The aircraft came to a halt and immediately the engines started to run down, cockpit open, my erk on the wing ready to help me remove my harnesses, leaving the machine tidy for its next duty. One of our Sergeants came over making sure all was well asking me.

"Enjoy your trip Merchant."

"Thank you Sergeant, fill her up will you. I may take her for another spin later."

Ian jumped out laughing at the same time pushing his thick dark hair back ruffled by his flying helmet.

"That was fun, did you enjoy it?" He asked.

"Yes sir. What was the airfield and why upside down?" I asked.

"Kenley, always do a slow roll over Kenley, birth place of 615., in 1937."
He replied.
I giggled thinking. *That's the sort of thing I would do. Sod who I was to
upset.* Walking across the grass back to the aircrew room I had a real
admiration for my pilot. Having coffee with the other pilots completed this
wonderful experience. They were special people who took interest in the
young cadets welfare promoting the fellow well met environment. Through
the aircrew window I could see Ron Fairhurst and Pee Wee Judge walking
towards the T7. It was Ron's turn to have the ride of his life and with such
a famous test pilot. I turned to Ian, my pilot, saying I had to wish my friend
well, could I be excused. Fear ran though my veins as I reached for my 120
box camera from my kit bag. Sod it I thought. I Had to get a shot of this
magical moment. I ran across the grass to the T7. I got it.

Photo: © Pilots Pals

Meteor MkT7 VW428
Flt. Lt. Pee Wee Judge can just be seen through the side canopy.
AC 2 Ron Fairhurst being strapped in by one of our famous erks.

I waved Ron goodbye hoping my friend would enjoy his experience as
much as I had earlier that special day. Thirty minutes later the T7 was back
with one very happy young man. Time to talk, share our experiences, we
were now in a position to bore the pants of the entire squadron. Returning
to the crew room, spending time with the other pilot, gave me a feeling of
enormous wealth to be sharing time with my heroes. Then yet another Mars
bar stuck sideways when the boss suggested we should attend the squadrons
two week summer camp in Malta, when we could get more flying in. This

world I was in had endless possibilities for priceless fun. Ron and I thanked "Bob" but we had to get ATC. approval for such a trip, knowing we had no chance. Back at 56 Woolwich we made application for the Malta attachment and was immediately turned down by Commanding Officer Flt. Lt. Watling.

"All overseas trips had to be authorised by Wing H.Q. London. You have no chance." He said.

The following weekend back at Biggin Hill I informed the boss of the outcome of my meeting with our C.O. at 56. His only reply was

"Next year we will play it different, carry on with your duties."

I saluted and left his office reporting to the duty Sergeant.

"What's your problem Merchant?" Asked the Sergeant.

"I have been refused permission to attend summer camp with the squadron and to be honest I'm a little fed up." I replied.

"Shame, it's fun in Malta." He said handing me my smelly's for the day.

Summer, winter. Life was one exciting game of aviation although not all ran smoothly with the squadron operations. On one occasion I was sitting on the grass watching four Meteors making ready for an exercise. Engines started , They're off, check brakes. The aircraft directly in front of our small group just kept coming,

"He's leaving it a bit JESUS," screamed an erk.

The aircraft failed to turn making me and some erks move faster than one would normally expect. The nose wheel had partially retracted when the aircraft came to a halt on the grass where we had been sitting. Outcame the pilot to the cheering and hand clapping of the other aircrew. The embarrassed pilot removed his helmet and standing in the cockpit and bowed to acknowledge his increasing audience. The scene reminded me of a great musician completing his finest performance, the more he bowed the louder his audience became. This was not the first time I had experienced the R.A.F. spirit. I was very proud to have witnessed these special moments with these special people of the Royal Auxiliary Air Force. Now the ground crews had the problem of making the aircraft serviceable. The first thing was to get the Meteor off the grass onto the apron, then the nose wheel in the fully down and locked position. It came off the grass with the efforts of all but how could the nose wheel be positioned correctly with all that weight on it. One of our very large Sergeants stepped forward with his finger in the air, as to say leave it to me chaps. He jumped on the inner wing and proceeded to cat walk, on all fours, down the fuselage toward the rear of the aircraft, over the aerial to reach the tail and yes the weight of our mighty NCO enabled the rest of the crew to secure the nose wheel fully down and locked. Another big cheer and clapping for the team. Now our proud mighty Sergeant put himself in reverse, no way could such a giant turn on such a small area, until his rear met with all his weight into the forgotten aerial. Straight up and eyebrows to follow the aerial penetrated the R.A.F. blue lower garment of our hero, eyes watering the Sergeant tried to remove the offensive spike. I laughed and laughed feeling helpless to aid the victim of this hilarious situation.

Flight Safety.
"ALWAYS CHECK YOUR HYDRAULIC LEVELS" Not with the Meteors aerial.

Photo: © Pilots Pals

Flt. Lt. Hugh Merewether completing his walk round prior to a sortie South East Apron, Biggin Hill, 1955

Flt Lt Hugh Merewether left 615 Squadron during 1955 to become a test pilot for Hawker, where his former Squadron Commander, Neville Duke was the chief test pilot flying the Hawker Hunter. Another of my hero's that I never had the opportunity to meet.

Sqn. Ldr. Tommy Evans of 609 Squadron receives the Esher Trophy from Sqn. Ldr. Bob Eeles from the back seat of the Mk. T7

The winner of the Esher Trophy 1954 was 609 Squadron R.Aux.A.F. based at R.A.F. Church Fenton. During 1955 615 Squadron flew 4 Meteors, 3 Mk 8's and a Mk.T7 from Biggin for the hand-over of this competitive trophy.

A brief history of the Esher Trophy

This magnificent trophy was founded by Viscount Esher in 1926. It is a bronze figure, sculpted by Sir Alfred Gilbert, of Perseus on an ornate base. The trophy was awarded each year for squadron efficiency within the Royal Auxiliary Air Force. The full history of this trophy and the 21 auxiliary squadrons can be found in Leslie Hunt's book "Twenty One Squadrons". It was during my research about this trophy that I had the pleasure of having contact with David Darley, the news letter Editor of 609 Squadron Association. The whereabouts of the trophy had featured in their magazine, Tally-Ho. Our conversation gave David more determination to locate its final resting place. A week or so later David e-mailed me to say he had located it in the archives of the R.A.F. Museum, Hendon in a wooden box. I shall explain later my disappointment at this news.

Left is Fl. Lt Hugh Merewether . Right. The smiling Fl. Lt. Dickey Reed.
Behind the Land Rover became Dillow's Café, A.K.A. The Greasy Spoon.

Photos : © Pilots Pals

The aircrew relaxing in the in the summer sun, me incorrectly dressed, it
was far too warm for the issued smellies. The R.A.F. Coach parked in the
background is on the site of what was the Steel House until 19th June 2012.

Summer camp 1956 R.A.F. St Athan, Wales. Not the best of stations to spend a week but better than nothing. The station was a maintenance training unit rather than the usual operational squadron base so it could not offer the active station experience of the previous year at Duxford with its two squadrons of Meteors. However, at St Athan we were accommodated in wooden huts rather than being under canvas at Duxford.

56 Squadron ATC. 1956 Summer camp. R.A.F. St. Athan, Wales.

I'm back row third from the left. Note the dog collar, uncomfortable, sore in the winter, hot in the summer. The accommodation allowed us to be smart at all times. Shine on your boots not having to step out into a mud patch and a uniform that was not damp in the mornings holding its crease until midday. Trousers were placed under the mattress of one's bed in the hope body weight would provide a good crease the following morning. I'm limited telling you all that went on during this week but we did have some fun. One story I can tell. The adjacent hut accommodated young air force erks, not the best people you want to meet, in fact a very miserable lot. We removed a fire extinguisher from the their hut without them knowing. Later that night we placed it at the correct angle to their door. One of our chaps would bang on the door as hard as possible shouting *"fire fire."* Hit the fire extinguisher trigger and run as fast as possible. Erk opens the door to be met by a face full of foam. Brilliant! The subsequent enquiry had little evidence so we all had a good laugh at those unsociable erks. Back to Biggin Hill for me.

The name Eeles has a long and continuing connection with the Royal Air Force. Bob's uncle, a Sqn .Ldr H. Eeles took command of 263 Squadron June 1940 eventually to retire from the R.A.F. as an Air Commodore. During 1955 I saw a young boy dressed in a grey school uniform aged about 12 talking to Bob. Half an hour later the lad was flying in the T7. I was to learn later he was the nephew of our Boss; lucky boy to have such an uncle. Forty years later I was to meet that young gentleman once again. More later.

Photo: Via Dan Graham

F.O Ian Smith   Sqn. Ldr "Bob" Eeles   Flt Lt. Peter Pledger
Flt. Lt Pee Wee Judge   Flt. Lt. Mike D'Arcy   Flt. Lt. Tony Vivian

I travelled to Biggin each Saturday so that I could attend my own ATC. Squadron on Sundays. I was doing wrong but why should I say anything to anyone. I had such a rich life and was not willing to allow anyone to interfere. My journey back to R.A.F. Kidbrook could be lonely but it gave me time to think of my second love, Margaret, who I had lost in the autumn of the previous year. I lost the greatest friend in my life, a pain that was to repeat itself many times in my life. Love hurts, don't it. More time spent with the aircrew and then Bob told me that when I was 17 I should apply for transfer to the Royal Auxiliary Air Force. May 1957 could not come fast enough. Merchant Erk. Think of it, my own smelly's.   .

41 Squadron's Hunters with 600's Meteors _{Photo: Via Dan Graham}

There was a time when both the Biggin Hill based auxiliary squadrons were looking forward to receiving the Hawker Hunter as a replacement for their Meteors, but it was never to be.

560647, AC2 Merchant J. J. _{Photo: © Pilots Pals}

Incorrectly dressed in R.A.F blue shirt, black tie, beret tucked in my trousers. I felt the richest young man in the world.

It must have been late February 1957 when I was called to the Boss' office. Sqn. Lrd R. Eeles, "Bob", informed me that the squadron was due to be disbanded and I should no longer attend R.A.F. Biggin Hill. He extended his hand, I paused too long,

"Goodbye Merchant." He said in a very firm commanding voice.

I offered my weak hand and suddenly realising my position gave this great man a firm hand shake, took one step back and saluted my farewell. Collecting my belongings I found myself leaning against the hangar side door, cold, and angry . I had to run, I needed to replace this emotion with physical pain I ran as fast as I could. Seeing a 410 bus I jumped on not understanding my actions. Why, why. I could not have faced my colleagues at the squadron. I could not say goodbye. Run, get away. I remember it started to rain, the weather had turned dull, chilly and damp. That night I laid on my bed coming to terms with such emotional pain. First Margaret, now 615, these emotions were to last for many years. I had lost so many good friends. Thinking back I now realise how extremely fortunate I was to have had the opportunity denied to the youth of today. I had been in the right place at the right time.

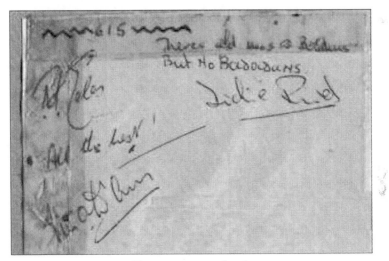

From my scrap book.

Sqd. Ldr R. Eeles, Flt. Lt. D Reed, Flt Lt. M D'Arcy

A frequent sight over South East England during the 1950's

Not too sure of the date of this photograph but you may notice the pilots are still wearing the old leather helmets before being issued with the Mk1 silver Bone Dome with blue cloth interior.

Photos: Via Dan Graham

1957

Royal Air Force Biggin Hill. 10th March 1957 the last day of the Royal Auxiliary Air Force. 600 and 615 Squadron's Meteors Mk 8

A proud day for R.A.F. Biggin Hill &
The Station Commander   Photo: Via Dan Graham

From a single Hurricane LF363, (based at R.A.F. Biggin Hill and the last of
its type in R.A.F. Service) and the enthusiasm of the Station Commander,
Wing Commander Peter Thompson DFC. grew what is now known interna-
tionally as the "Battle of Britain Memorial Flight". The new flight although
officially approved was not to receive public funding. All necessary work
had to be voluntary thereby creating an enormous challenge for the R.A.F.

In 1957 the R.A.F. phased out the Spitfire leaving only the 3 PR XIX's
examples being flown by the "Temperature & Humidity Monitoring Flight"
based at R.A.F. Woodvale. These aircraft joined the lone Hurricane at R.A.F.
Biggin Hill on the 11th July, 1957, for the official launch ceremony of the
new flight named "Historic Aircraft Flight". Affectionately known as "BoB
Flight" by Wing Commander Thompson.

The above photograph taken on that day at West Camp, H.Q. of 41 Squad-
ron includes: Hurricane LF363, 3 Spitfires PM631 - PS853 - PS915, 3
Hunters from 41 Squadron and 3 Javelins from 46 Squadron based at R.A.F.
Odiham.

In 1958 the "Historic Aircraft Flight" was moved to R.A.F. North Weald and
renamed the flight to "Battle of Britain Flight". It became the "Battle of
Britain Memorial Flight" in June 1969.

Chapter 4

Chapter 5

The emotional impact of any loss will inevitably change a young life, both mentally and physically. In my case I rebelled against authority without truly understanding all that surrounded me. I made mistakes I would live to regret. Looking back I should have spent my energy on constructive thinking and left behind what was and has now gone forever.

Joseph J. Merchant 1989

Filling my time with night school and the cadets got me through this bad time though to be honest though, I was lonely. I had now started work going from job to job until I found happiness serving my time working in New Eltham for W. F. Stanley & Co. Ltd. This famous instrument makers gave me good work companionship and a moderate salary. My first pay packet was £4.15s. 50% for Mum and 50% for me. I was wealthy.

April 1957 and I felt I had to return to Biggin Hill. I don't know why but I cycled one Saturday morning not knowing what I would find. Through the back way to my old squadron I peered through the locked hangar doors the Meteors were parked as the erk's had always left them, all was still. I looked across the airport to the north east at 600's hangar, all so very quiet. My eyes drifted to the west camp. 41 Squadron were still operating their Hunters but being a weekend all the aircraft were hangared. The memories came flooding back, the people those special people dispersed like broken pieces of porcelain never to be one unit again. The corner of our hangar brought a smile to my face, my mind going back to our Flt. Sergeant placing me on a charge for being cheeky. Punishment, sweeping out the hangar. Jesus I thought that's going to take all day. The Sergeant's instructions came clear.
"You start here and work your way to the other end."
Then to my astonishment he handed me a toothbrush, making it very clear that this must be completed within a month shouting *"Get on with it."*
The times I looked at that corner of the hangar and smiled thinking of those wonderful people. The Government defence budget cuts gave the R.Aux.A.F. a few weeks to disband. The servicemen of the Royal Auxiliary Airforce Squadrons had responsibilities, wives, families and mortgages. Suddenly the financial carpet was pulled from under their feet leaving most of the men angry. They had given up their week ends and their holidays period for those squadrons. Only two years earlier Sir Winston Churchill praised and thanked all the members of 615 for their devotion to duty in maintaining Britain's air power. Closure of the Auxiliaries could have been handled in a far better way. However, we see the hand of the dreaded 'bean counter' at work. Whatever the industry or service you may work for never lose sight of this creature. Ruthless, unashamed and evil, they will strike with their pencils not having the conscience of a hangman. I remember a wonderful quotation from one of our industrialists back in the 60's, and I quote.
"Accountants are the barnacles on the ship's arse of progress."
Poetry, pure bloody poetry.

I returned home that Saturday feeling lost and lonely again, I should have realised the visit would only bring pain, frustration and more sadness. I had to think positive for my future so I continued with my much loved ATC. activities that gave me many hours of fun with my many new friends. I purchased a 500cc Matchless motor bike with sidecar. Why? I don't know, it seemed a good idea at the time. My good friend Ron Fairhurst had his BSA Bantam volunteered to teach me to ride this beast. Once you had the thing started it resembled a tractor, one thud from the piston gave you 20 feet of travel. All documentation completed, I walked this beast down to Ron's house where he took charge assuring me it was a piece of cake. Off we went, going straight no problem, then we came to our first corner. Ron turned the handle bars, nothing, we mounted the curb ploughing our way through an old lady's fence and then onto her garden. Ron was sitting on the petrol tank while I was sitting in the riders saddle The engine was still giving its reassuring thud as the old lady appeared waving her fist.

"Time to get out of here Ron." I said as we both gathered our strength to remove the beast back onto the road. I sold it the next day for £5.00 at the loss of £20.00.

56 Squadron ATC 1957 Summer camp R.A.F. Leuchars.

R.A.F. Leuchars. An operational base with 43(F) and 111(F) Squadrons operating the Hunter. We had rifle shooting, flying and Air Sea Rescue gave us a thrill in their high speed launch powered by two Merlin engines, that was some ride. Last day of camp gave me a brilliant flight in the Chipmunk. Upside down over the River Tay. Corporal Joe Merchant was a happy lad.

I returned to Biggin on the odd occasion, nose through the fence again, with very little movement from 41 Squadron. The news that R.A.F Biggin Hill was to be closed as an operational unit was to be expected. Between the 16th and the 30th of January 1958 41 Squadron was disbanded reforming on 1st February at R.A.F. Coltishall flying the Gloster Javelin. I honestly thought this was to be the end of a great era in my life. WRONG.

Photo: © David Webster

41 Squadron's Hunters the last fighters at R.A.F. Biggin Hill

I do believe the R.A.F. at one time, had plans for Biggin Hill. Yes, they had stopped all flying but WWII German aircraft started to arrive from R.A.F. St Athan and were being assembled in one hangar on West Camp. It was July 1957 at R.A.F. Biggin Hill when the R.A.F. formed the now world famous Battle of Britain Memorial Flight with 1 Hurricane and 3 Spitfires. The new Chapel St Georges Chapel of Remembrance had been dedicated in November 1951. As a young enthusiast I thought these events were all pointing to a future museum that surely Biggin Hill should have to celebrate the victory in the "Battle of Britain". What better place to acknowledge the price paid by our boys and girls during those dark days. Sir Winston Churchill once said Biggin Hill will never close. It is a well known fact that this statesman had a special place in his heart for this airfield, he knew that had the R.A.F. failed during 1940 all would have been lost. Allowing the Germans the upper hand ready for the invasion of England. He took the aircrews as friends, one I can confirm was Sqn. Ldr Neville Duke whose first posting to Biggin Hill was in 1941 with 92 squadron. In 1948 Duke joined 615 Sqn R.Aux.A.F. becoming their C.O. 1950 -1951. I am convinced had Churchill not suffered a stroke in 1955, that unfortunately forced him to retire as Prime Minister, Biggin Hill would have had its true value recognised by making it the official Battle of Britain Museum. No, it was not to be, somebody had influence. The WWII German aircraft hangered on West Camp were dismantled and transported to an R.A.F. storage depot. The heart breaking thought that the future museums were to be R.A.F. Hendon and R.A.F. Cosford. What the hell R.A.F. Hendon had to do with the Battle of Britain, only Christ knows.

Vickers Wellington T10 MF628

Photos: © George Baczkowski

Messerschmitt Bf 110G-4/R-6

A few examples of the many WW 11 aircraft stored at R.A.F. Biggin Hill.

Chapter Five

Summer camp for 1958 was R.A.F. St Evel, Cornwall a Coastal Command base operating Shackletons and where the cadets experienced flying many hours over the Atlantic. I was lucky, my trip was a local with some circuits and bumps, a good experience but very boring after so many hours. The countryside and coast line around the base was so beautiful, my first time in these parts of England and gave me views I had never experienced. Most of the coast line that I remember was rugged with rough seas. Saturday soon came round and we were on our way back to London. I was feeling a bit sorry for myself as I had thoroughly enjoyed the station and the surrounding environment and had no wish to return home.

I purchased a second-hand 1939 AJS 350cc ex military motorcycle equipped with girder forks and solid rear frame. It also had the first automatic cut off system, when it rained it stopped. What with my own transport and hairs growing on my arms Mother nature was preparing me for manhood. Bloody frightening I had bills to pay, so this is manhood? Road Tax, Insurance, Petrol, Pension? I've just come out of nappies and Mum and Dad are pushing me to invest in a pension, okay one shilling a week, that's all I was willing to invest. We had a bloody atomic war hanging over our heads and Mum and Dad want me to invest in the future, what future?

It was a wonderful time. Bill Haley had gone into clocks and de Havilland named a aeroplane after his backing group, things were really looking up. Everything seemed to fall into place, the summers were warm and the winters were cold. I was under the impression that all politicians were farmers due to the amount of bullshit they came out with, not that I truly understood politics at this age and yet I still idolized Churchill knowing his connection with 615 Squadron and R.A.F. Biggin Hill. During my Auxiliary days I met a Flight Lieutenant who told me Churchill never paid his mess bills when popping into the Officers' Mess at Biggin. These visits must have been frequent as Biggin was on his way home from London. His bar bill had to be divided among the unfortunate officers stationed there.

"Never in the mess has so much been consumed by so few and paid for by so many."

Arriving very late at our ATC HQ's one Sunday morning there must have been 60 cadets waiting for the building to be opened. Realizing I was the senior NCO there I moved the group into the old polytechnic grounds clearing the pavement. On arrival of our Commanding Officers he congratulated me on using my initiative snd with immediate affect I was promoted to a Sergeant and he apologised for not giving spare keys to the senior NCO. Within 6 months I was promoted to Flight Sergeant and immediately applied for a new uniform that was granted by W.O. Gauge. The issue of most equipment was far from your size relying on your Mum to deal with the necessary alterations, I would go one better than that by delivering my new uniform to the Royal Artillery tailor in Wellington Street for fitting. Many Officers and ranks from the Royal Artillery barracks had their uniforms tailored by this master tailor. The result was very comfortable fit plus having a permanent seam machined into my trouser crease.

Photo: © Flt. Lt. J. Watling

R.A.F. Hullavington 1959 Summer camp. The 56 Sqn. NCO's.

Sgt. M. Fox	Cadet W/O A. Hogg	Clp. Ayton	Sgt. M. Bowtle
	Flt. Sgt. J. Merchant	Cpl. S Pledge	

More Chipmunk flying plus a wonderful experience in a Vickers Varsity used by the R.A.F. for navigation training. This aircraft was fitted with a prone position on the underside of the fuselage so each cadet had the opportunity of a face down view of the county-side flying by. Some, though, found this a little disturbing and rejected the offer. I loved every minute fantasising I was flying on my own.

I was, to put it very mildly, a bit of a rebel. I found myself critical of a few things, plus a new emotion, one perhaps that had been with me for some years but I had not truly understood. The first thing I rebelled against, apart from Dad's strict discipline, was my poppy, worn during remembrance week. After reading some of the battles of WWI I became obsessed with hatred for the people responsible for our loss of, what I saw, a future generation of fine English men, poets, musicians, engineers and possible statesmen. Who were these irresponsible morons that sent so many of our people to their early graves. The more I read the more I became aware of the words in the centre of my poppy, 'Earl Haig Fund'. Field Marshal D. Haig, in my book this person was one big war criminal. Born within the wealth of the Haig whisky company he had a charmed life enjoying such luxuries as a good education and no money problems. Good luck to anybody having such a great start in life but for an outdated cavalry officer to be given the responsibility for the British Expeditionary Force from 1915 until the end of the war was a big mistake. Mistakes continued to be made throughout WWI leading to British loss of some 662,000 dead, 140,000 missing presumed dead and 1.6 million wounded.

I have never truly studied the campaigns of this tragic period of British history and I have to accept that the losses by France and too the Central Powers far exceeded our own. However, it beggars belief that our High Command should have so recklessly committed the British infantry to such enormous casualty rates. Nevertheless on his return to England Haig was made an Earl, evidence of much white washing, with even more to come when he was given a state funeral in 1928. The big problem with white wash it doesn't last very long and the underlying facts will eventually show through. He did set up the 'Earl Haig Fund' giving rise to his name appearing on the Remembrance Day Poppies; a matter that ranked with many, myself included. As a 18 years old I rebelled in the only way I could. Dismantling my poppy, I would place the silver wrapper from my Kit-Kat over the black centre 'Haig Fund', never was I told to remove it by our NCO's or Officers in the many years I wore the uniform. This practice continued until The British Legion removed the word Haig. I like to think my letter to this organisation played a small part in removing his name forever.

This emotion gave birth to a new word in my vocabulary. Apsole. I dislike the use of bad language in public so should somebody fail to meet a reasonable standard he/she was a Apsole; meaning, nasty person, Litter lout, Accountant, Politician, Bully, Dictator, Solicitor. When I refer to a standard I refer those who that give a lot and expect little in return. The Apsoles of this world are not totally bad, just 99% bad, so avoid them at all costs.

Photo: © Fl. Lt Watlin

56 Squadron Air Training Corps

This foot/rifle drill might be viewed with some criticism for allowing young cadets to handle arms. However, this small part of our training welded the cadets into a cohesive squadron; demonstrated by the frequency that 56 were successful in winning the wing competitions. Over the many years that have passed I have maintained contact with four of these cadets

The parade ground on which we trained formed the original entrance to the Woolwich Polytechnic and was situated at the rear of our headquarters in Wellington Street.

Chapter Five

Chapter 6

Returning to an active Biggin Hill initially prompted some doubts because of the very strange and unfriendly people. They say never go back you will be disappointed. Going back, though, with flying opportunities painted a new picture. It was time for me to start getting my enthusiastic feet under the table with the many different young and old characters that had settled here from Croydon..

Joseph J. Merchant 1990

West Camp 1959

Photo: © Norman Rivett

1970's

Biggin Hill Airport was divided into two on January 1st 1959. West Camp with the western taxi way, clearly seen in these photos which would create problems in the future, remained under the control of the M.o.D. This residual R.A.F. Station, then became the home of the Air Crew Selection Centre. The Eastern side was leased to Surrey Aviation who had moved from Croydon. Note the new entrance to the control tower from Main Road.

Date.	Aircraft.		Captain.	Holder's Operating Capacity.	Journey or Nature of Flight.			FLYING TI		
	Type.	Markings.			From	To		Departure	Arrival	Day. In Charge.
21-12-58	HAWK TRAINER III. G-AKAS		SELF	Instr.	CROYDON	LOCAL		15.25	16.15	00.50
26-12-58	HAWK TRAINER III. G-AKAS		SELF	Instr.	CROYDON	LOCAL		11.45	12.10	00.25
27-12-58	HAWK TRAINER III. G-AITN		SELF	Instr.	CROYDON	LOCAL		11.05	12.35	01.30
27-12-58	HAWK TRAINER III. G-AITN		SELF	Instr.	CROYDON	LOCAL		12.55	13.30	00.35
27-12-58	HAWK TRAINER III. G-AITN		SELF	Instr.	CROYDON	LOCAL		14.25	15.35	01.10
28-12-58	HAWK TRAINER III. G-AKAS		SELF	Instr.	CROYDON	LOCAL		11.30	11.50	00.20
28-12-58	HAWK TRAINER III. G-AKAS		SELF	Instr.	CROYDON	LOCAL		14.00	15.00	01.00
29-12-58	HAWK TRAINER III. G-AKAS		SELF	Instr.	CROYDON	LOCAL		15.35	16.15	00.40
30-12-58	HAWK TRAINER III. G-AITN		SELF	Instr.	CROYDON	LOCAL		11.55	12.00	00.25
30-12-58	HAWK TRAINER III. G-AKAS		SELF	Instr.	CROYDON	LOCAL		12.30	12.50	00.20
30-12-58	HAWK TRAINER III. G-AITN		SELF	P.1	CROYDON	LOCAL		15.35	16.10	00.35
3-1-59	HAWK TRAINER III. G-AKAS		SELF	P.1	CROYDON	BIGGIN HILL		11.05	11.20	00.15

Flying instructor Rex Nicholls log book.

Photo: © Rex Nicholls

The E.F.G. Flying Club Hawk Trainer Mk 111 G-AKAS

3rd January 1959. Rex Nicholls and student Frankie O'Kane were the first civilians to use Biggin Hill Airport. The official hand over date was the 1st January 1959. The air traffic control remained in the hands of the Royal Air Force for a short time.

Date	Aircraft		Captain or 1st Pilot	2nd Pilot, Pupil or Passenger	Details of Flight
	Type	Registration			
14TH DEC 1958	M65 GEMINI 1A	G-AJWF	W WEBB.	SELF	LOCAL SOUTH.
28TH DEC 58	TIGER MOTH	G-ANKB	D PERCH.		TAKE OFF LANDINGS.
4 JAN 59	" "	"	G STEWART.		" "
16TH JAN 59	C.P-301 LINNET	G-APNS	NEVILLE DUKE		FAMILARIZATION
15TH FEB 59	TIGER MOTH	G-ANKB	L ROYLE		CROSS COUNTRY
		CROYTON CLOSED	DORDN /		
26TH APR 59	TIGER MOTH	EI-AGR	G DONOHOE	SELF	CIRCUITS + BUMPS.
9TH MAY 59	" "	EI-AGR	"	"	" "
10TH MAY 59	" "	EI-AGR	CAPT KENNEDY.	"	" "

Grand total, excluding passenger flying........ 19 ....hours.... 40 ....minutes

The flying log of the then student pilot Derek White 1958/59 confirming the closure of Croydon. The pilots in command of his training had already made their names in aviation; Bill Webb, Don Perch and Neville Duke.

Photo: © Rex Nicholls

South East area

This photo was taken in 1959 by Rex Nicholls . The black hangar in the background was 615 HQ, now Jet Aviation. The buildings right of centre were the old fire station demolished 2008. The hut in front was the EFG club house. The foreground area was Doug Arnold's, then GoldAir. The two roads becoming, Churchill Way left and Wireless Road right.

Chapter Six

During the spring of 1959 I returned to Biggin Hill just to be nosy and perhaps reminisce a little. Life had been made easier travelling around Kent on my 350 AJS provided it didn't rain. Riding past the guard room I smiled thinking of our friendly Sergeant and wondered if his Mother in Law continued her weekend visits. The beautiful remembrance chapel with its gate guardians, a Hurricane and a Spitfire, plus the neatly cared for garden. All this still had a special place in my heart. Coming up to the traffic lights at the end of runway 03, lights permanently on green, I saw a light aircraft making an approach for landing, suddenly from the cockpit something white fell into the upper valley woods. I parked the bike and ran down through the woods to find a white flying helmet. Opportunity knocks, I thought. So back on the bike with the flying helmet stuffed in my black riding jacket I entered the airfield through the old south camp entrance, which now appeared to be permanently open with no fence or gate. The airfield was much the same as I had left it back in '57. except for a few private aircraft parked around the south camp. I couldn't find aircraft or pilots but continued my search looking at this familiar environment now in very different hands.

The South East Camp was scruffy, not as I had left it. The grass had been neglected, the apron had weeds growing in the joints in the concrete and cars were parked all over the place. Returning to the South Camp a sign 'Air Touring Flying Club' caught my attention. I parked the bike and climbed the stairs to the entrance, opened the door to be met by silence, not a word was said. No hi, hello, good morning. What a miserable bunch of people, how unfriendly can you get, flying club, it was more like a dying club. Eventually one chap came up to me saying

"Can I help you?"

It was immediately obvious this gentleman had a mammoth social problem. I had to remember who I was, a Mr. Nobody.

"I retrieved this flying helmet from the woods about 15 minutes ago and I cannot find the aircraft or its pilot." I replied.

A possible Apsole I thought.

"I'll make sure the pilot gets it back."

He responded and turned his back on me. No thank you, nothing. Confirmed, we have an Apsole. I have to be honest I felt very embarrassed and left the premises as quickly as possible. I never did find out who he was nor did I ever return to that very unfriendly club. After making a few enquiries I was to learn that Croydon had closed transferring all its movements to Biggin Hill. Following is a brief report on the final moments of Croydon.

On 30th September 1959, after an eventful life of some 44 years, Croydon Airport was to finally close. By the time the final scheduled flight arrived - a Morton Airways de Havilland Dove from Newmarket - a sizable crowd had gathered to witness the last sad moment of this once great airport.

As the famous clock on the control tower showed 18.39 the final scheduled flight departed. It was another Morton Airways aircraft, a de Havilland Heron bound for Rotterdam. Ironically, the pilot was Captain Last. Soon after the few remaining airliners also departed - empty - and the crowd began to disperse. Very few took notice of a small bonfire by the hangar some way from the main terminal buildings and hangars. On top of the bonfire was an effigy of the Minister of Transport, the final gesture of the protesters who had fiercely opposed the closure of Croydon Airport.

Among the protesters was Christopher de Vere, later to become the first Secretary of the Croydon Airport Society, it was almost dusk when he climbed into his Miles Gemini, G-AJWE. As he sped across the grass runway the sound if its engines echoed eerily in the empty hangars. The final aircraft to leave Croydon was bound for Biggin Hill.

My flying hours had reached 11 hours 30 minutes, most flights being in my favourite aircraft the Chipmunk a type I had learned to love and respect. On 31st January 1960 56 ATC Squadron were allocated a days Chipmunk flying at R.A.F. West Malling. As the senior NCO on duty I had to ensure that junior cadets flew first incase the weather turned. This day was clear, sunny, but very cold and time was getting on but with the three Chipmunks operating all cadets had flown 30 minutes each it would now be my turn. Parachute on I walked, well shuffled, towards the running aircraft. To my great surprise I saw that the pilot was Smiffy, Flying Officer Ian Smith, the pilot from 615 that flew me in a Meteor some 3 years previously. Once strapped in with headset on I presented myself.

"Good afternoon sir I'm Flt. Sgt. Joseph Merchant ex 615 attachment, you flew me in the T7 back in 1955."
I said, trying so hard not to sound too excited.
"Well I never, how are you." he replied.
"Stand by, I'll call the tower"
Ian called and permission was given for taxing to the runway.
"You were saying." he continued

"All has been fine sir but I miss 615 and always will. Do you see any of the other pilots, Pee wee, Bob?" I asked.

"Not that often but we stay in touch. We're all so very busy these days, 615 was our meeting point and when that went so did our point of contact. Stand by, I have to talk to the tower."

Permission was given for take off and Ian didn't waste a second to get his aircraft in the air.

"How much time do you have on the Chipmunk." He asked.

"Just over five hours sir." I replied.

"Well lets see what we can achieve today, would you like to do some aerobatics?" He asked.

"Yes please sir." I replied.

While climbing to 3000 feet it gave us a chance to talk over the old Biggin Hill days. Once at 3,000 feet Ian talked me through several aerobatic manoeuvres. By now I was well used to the G effects being pushed into ones seat or being inverted hanging in the straps.

"Go through a loop with me and then see if you can complete one yourself" he said.

"Yes please sir." I replied excitedly.

"Right, take the control column, not too tight, bank to the right, watch your nose, don't let it fall, now straight and level, bank to the left, that's very good you didn't let that nose fall well done. Put your hand on the throttle applying full power push the stick forward, look at your air speed indicator, 120 knots, pull the stick back, keep going and over she goes. Good, now watch your slip and turn once you have applied full power, stick forward, 120 on the clock pull back, good, ease off, good, straight and level, well done. How do you feel?" He inquired.

"Wonderful sir, truly wonderful, one more before returning." I asked."

"Okay, one more, together and then home." He said.

Returning to West Malling gave me the opportunity to talk to Ian regarding my continuing yearning to fly. National Service had come to an end, one hell of a mistake by the Government, ending any chance of flying with the R.A.F. even as a erk.

"You can do it, you have just proved that." He said.

"Thank you for this wonderful opportunity sir, I shall make a special note in my log book, thanks again sir, bye."

Walking away from the still running aircraft I looked back to wave my farewell. Ian responded with a thumbs up and the soundless words.

"Good luck"

R.A.F. West Malling January 1960. F/O Ian Smith & myself

I returned to Biggin Hill but the camaraderie had gone, people were no longer friendly, I found it strange to be on Biggin surrounded by aircraft and not have the buzz of happiness. I guess the entire commercial world is the same regardless of its industry. Back at Woolwich with 56 the fun continued, it seemed to be an endless source of laughter, why did we laugh so much and more importantly at what.?

The sudden introduction of a new civilian instructor to 56 was a breath of fresh air. Tony Wilcox who flew at Biggin Hill with the Surrey & Kent Flying Club. Tony, soon to be Flying Officer Wilcox, since he had passed an A.T.C. examination board for a commission. He had applied to the R.A.F. but been turned down twice on medical grounds. The success of his third application would depend on the outcome of surgery on a nasal problem. All being well the R.A.F. would take him for flying duty. Tony received his VR commission winning the respect of all the cadets, his ability to instruct left our other staff members well behind, he did have the charm that made one feel comfortable in his company either training or at our social meetings that gathered momentum, particularly on Friday nights after our parade.

16th February 1960 I was promoted to the newly introduced ATC rank of cadet Warrant Officer. I believe this was introduced to allow cadets to continue beyond their 20th birthday

During 1961 Tony flew the senior NCO's of 56 Squadron from Biggin Hill to the Isle of White. It was a very uncomfortable bumpy flight.

Photo: © Pilots Pals

Flt Sgt Martin Bowtle - W/O Alan Hogg - W/O Joe Merchant
Percival Prentice G-AOMF. My first private flight from Biggin Hill

I was back flying at Biggin Hill but it was never to be the same. The only friendly person I met was Tony, but the trip to the Isle of Wight was a good experience of civilian flying for all the NCO's. The Prentice was one of four based at Biggin Hill, only G-APPL is still there. G-AOMF (VS316) sold and flown to New Zealand during the 1970's, reregistered ZK-DJC it is now in the Wanaka museum. G-AOKF (VR284) sold to Liberia 1966. G-AONB was operated by 600 Squadron Flying Group.

The last time I had seen those distinctive markings was in 1957 on the side of 600 Sqn. Meteors. The wings of NB were used on G-AOKZ now a static example at the Midland Air Museum.

Photo: © Iain MacKay

Auster 3 G-AHLK 1960

I remember seeing this aircraft in 1956 parked in the same position outside the office of the then Commanding Officer Sqd. Ldr "Bob" Eeles .that became the offices of the Surrey and Kent Flying club office in 1959. I also found it comical that the Auster wore the marking of the 615 Squadron on the door. Trying to locate a photograph of this machine, not having its registration, did take me sometime and it was pure luck that flying instructor Peter Oake sent me the Don Bullock photo collection. This contained the above photo with the heading "Pee Wee's Auster". I do believe Fl. Lt "Pee Wee" Judge used this as a hack rather than road transport.

During my research I found that 615 had continued its association with Biggin Hill. Flight magazine published a list of clubs and groups yearly and in their issue March 1960 under P. F.A. Co-ownership Groups and Clubs is listed 615 Flying Group, Biggin Hill.

Photos: © Brian Richards

Thinking back 615 did have some very famous and busy pilots, Pee Wee Judge, Hugh Merewether and the most famous of all Neville Duke. The Auster G-AHLK flies on a permit in her new colours coded NJ889 from Staveton.

Note the zigzags from 615 Sqn.

56 Air Training Corps was doing very well. The Squadron won almost all competitions that it entered, always under the guidance of W/O Sheridon. The Girls' Venture Corps was also very successful and sharing the same building was an advantage to both organisations. Unfortunately the young ladies were not recognised by the Royal Air Force (M.o.D.) so the costs of their training fell to fund raising and to the parents. Today, though, both male and female can join the Air Training Corps units throughout the UK.

1553 Unit Women's Junior Air Corps.

Left is a delightful young lady I went to junior school with, Rosemary. Far right is Lynne Field others, Liz Chilvers, Pauline Elliott. Mary Harris O.B.E. Unit leader holding yet another trophy. During 1964 the unit became The Girls Venture corps.

The time came for our friend Tony Wilcox to leave the private world of aviation and his duties with 56 Squadron. After his minor operation Tony passed his third medical for aircrew in the Royal Air Force. He was thrilled to think he would be financially rewarded for all his future flying rather than paying for the pleasure. His farewell party was one to remember when Tony told of his last flight in a Tiger Moth that Saturday morning.

"I taxied out to 23 grass and on take off noticed a group of people filming at the end of the runway; bloody dangerous I thought. I carried on with my flight to Rochester and on returning to Biggin Hill I noticed our brave camera crew were still working. Thinking I could give them a shot they will never forget I lined the Tiger up for a low level full throttle fly by. Initially I could see them frozen, just looking. Suddenly both crew and cameras went in all directions as I passed over them about 110 knots." After landing I thought I would join our filming friends to find out what they were up to and enquire whether they found their work somewhat dangerous?"

"If we get our hands on the stupid bastard that nearly killed us."
the boss replied.

"Dangerous, terribly dangerous." Tony said making his way towards the club bar. I was not to see Tony for two years due to his Royal Air Force training and later his overseas duties.

County's Tiger Moth G-ANKB   Photo: © Terry Kent
1st July 1961

Clean shaven Bob Needham with Roger Hardy and his Black Label Bentley parked on the airport, as we all did. *"Those were the days"*. As we all say.

Beware Aircraft Crossing

Auster 5 G-AKXP (NJ633). The Vendair hangar was situated on what is now the industrial estate. Crossing Churchill Way could be interesting.

Chapter Six

During this period I was on my own not attached to any particular club or organisation. However, just being on Biggin was enough to please me.

My research for this publication brought to light names that had slipped my mind and too the antics that made them well known on Biggin. Harry Harris acting C.F.I. for Vendair and County Flying Club and Charlie Vaughan, another pilot I would get to know, had obtained a couple of war surplus parachutes. They talked another pilot into flying them over the airport and with zero training they both jumped out. Local residents seeing the two 'chutes 'phoned the police informing them of an aeroplane crash . I never did find out what action was taken by the authorities, if any. This practice happened on more than one occasion during the early 60 s.

One well known character who had served in both world wars was Chris Draper, The Mad Major, well known for his feat in May 1953, of flying Auster G-AGYD under 15 of the 18 bridges spanning the River Thames. This was a publicity stunt to highlight that he was unemployed and broke. The next day a police officer knocked on his front door requesting his appearance at the local police station for a little chat. He was discharged by a magistrate court but ordered to pay Ten Guineas costs. Flight magazine's report on this incident May 1953 concluded and I quote *"We have no admiration for those busybodies who, on seeing the aircraft, hurried to telephone and volunteer information to the police."* Well said Flight. I was to meet him early 1960s when his license had been revoked by the Air Ministry who claimed his health was no longer up to pilots standards. His final remark to this order was:

"The crowning blow was that the revocation order was signed by a woman."

I met my favourite girlfriend, Margaret, again during the summer of 1961 having not seen or heard of her for five years. She looked as stunning as ever, now a fully developed woman with a smile that could sell tooth paste to a tramp. My attempt to win her emotions failed; she asked me to wait for a few more years, this I took as a big never. We parted as good friends but deep down her negative response hurt me. Although our relationship was healthy, on reflection I think I was suffering from natures' con, not understanding the difference between the brain and between the Y-Fronts. She was a good friend who would always have a special place in my heart. Back to Biggin Hill hiding my true feelings for my dearest friend. .

Photo: © Jerry Hughes

Experimental Flying Group Auster V

A beautiful shot of one of the many Auster's based at Biggin Hill in the 60s. Originally registered VR-LAF G-APRF registration was cancelled June 05.

Barry Wheeler (Scoop)

Barry Wheeler started his career with Flight International moving onto Airfix Ltd, M.o.D. & Key Publishing. Barry retired editor of Aviation News in 2009. He is photographed outside the EFG club house (Shed) early 1960s.

Photos: © Barry Wheeler

B-17G N5229V April 1962

One of the three B-17's flown to the UK for the film "The War Lover".This machine was scrapped together with N5232V later that year due to import duty required by the British Penguins. N9563Z returned to the U.S.A.

Percival Proctor IV G-ANXR

The Mk IV was used both as a 4 seat communication and 3 seat radio trainer by the R.A.F. RM221 has been on Biggin Hill since the early 1960s.

Photo: © Norman Rivett

Battle of Britain Day 16th September 1962

The Vulcan B2 XJ783 was from 83 Squadron that had taken delivery of their new aircraft only that year. 20 years later it was sold as scrap. The Tiger Moth G-AOBO was from the Surrey & Kent Flying Club taking advantage of advertising their services to the many thousands of enthusiasts that attended this R.A.F. at home that was a one day event held on the West Camp.

Once established in Biggin Hill the Surrey & Kent Flying Club's priority was their club house. Ben Parker, a very enthusiastic member, organised the removal of their club house from Croydon and its re-erection at Biggin Hill. I spent many lonely hours during this period as the new boy. Tony Wilcox introduced me to Jim Gibbs and a few other members of Surrey & Kent. One chap I did meet in these early days was a George Crew, Father of Dave Crew, who became another very keen flyer and later a private owner . Little did I think I would have such a long and happy association with the Crew family. It was around this time I bumped into a familiar face, Otto from 615. The name Otto due to his command of the German language, self taught I understood. It didn't take me long to realise he had completely lost the plot referring to me as Squadron Leader and insisting we return to Europe and finish the Reds off. Never did I think he would become a special person in my life. But he did. One great story I was to hear from the Surrey & Kent bar during this period was at a very late night drinking session, approximately 2.20 am, the club was raided by a group of police with their dogs. The members carried on with their conversations continuing to drink their ale when a very red face police office, obviously in charge, faced one of the members asking

"And what are you drinking sir."

the unexpected reply was

"That's very kind of you I'll have a half."

You can imagine the roar of laughter from the rest of the crew. Unfortunately the fine was £500.00 possibly due to the pilot's reply to a senior officer. Members clubbed together to ease the financial burden on the club.

Photo: © Norman Rivett

Battle of Britain Day 16th September. 1962

Parked next to the Vulcan on West Camp was Vickers Valiant KB1 XD874 of 148 Squadron as part of the Battle of Britain static display.

The Valiant was the first of the R.A.F.s trio of V Bombers followed by the Avro Vulcan and the Handley Page Victor. All three aircraft played a vital role in the U.K.'s strategic nuclear deterrent during the 60's. Development of this Vickers aircraft started in 1944 and the maiden flight was on 18th May 1951. 148 Squadron operated this type from July 1956 until April 1965.

Chapter Six

Chapter 7

Almost every turning in life involves money and this usually creates a delay with ones journey. The timing of my decision to learn to fly, September 1962, provided me with five months to prepare my financial position. There was little point spending time and money on light aviation during the English winter months. I therefore obtained the necessary books on navigation, meteorology and theory of flight, most of which I had studied with the ATC. With learning to fly always in my mind my reading was more of excitement than a chore. My commitment to working so diligently meant those winter months passed quickly. My longing ambition was in sight.

Joseph J. Merchant 1991

The formula of my past and the encouragement from so many friends now paved the way to my true ambition, to fly. My decision to learn to fly would cost me dear but be well worthwhile as I sought to fulfilling a dream. During the Autumn of 1962 I started to work all God's hours, not only at W. F. Stanley but also as a part time barman in the Sun in Sands pub in Blackheath. Little did I realise the valuable lessons this would provide later in my life. The pub was owned by an ex Army Major who insisted we should present ourselves as smart gentlemen wearing a uniform supplied by him. How right he was, the pub did very well under his command.

W. F. Stanley, New Eltham 1962. I was project supervisor for the Mk III Marching Compass contract we had from South Africa.

By the Spring of 1963 I had saved over £150 to cover the cost of flying a Chipmunk in aid of my private pilots licence. At that time the Chipmunk was the most expensive trainer on Biggin Hill @ £4.15 shillings per hour. But my experience with ATC flights made the Chipmunk the obvious choice . I was very happy with this machine, it fitted me wonderfully, like a new pair of Y-Fronts. In joining the Surrey & Kent Flying Club I knew I was walking in the footsteps of so many other pilots who had flown from the "Bump". Surely they too had experienced the same feeling of passion for aviation, or was I unique. My romantic thoughts soon vanished, disappearing into the till as I paid for my first lesson. In my humble opinion the first lesson was the worst trip I ever had. I learned very little from this so called air experience flight. By the second lesson I was getting bored with being flown around by different instructors learning sweet F/A (Aviation terminology meaning frightfully awful) Time to talk to the Chief Flying Instructor a certain Tiny Marshall. Now, to complete this task it was necessary to obtain a ladder, Tiny was 6'.4" with a voice to complement his build. He was the most understanding chap, I would say sympathetic with my complaints, but my next lesson was as bad as the rest, however time came for my first take off. We lined up on runway 29, following the instructors instructions I opened the throttle. Now at this very point I found out what the rudder

pedals are really for, so you can zigzag down the runway. Off the ground she came comparable to a Kangaroo at the height of a rut and only 80 degrees off our original heading. As we climbed out over 600 Squadron's old hanger I heard my instructor comment
"Thank God that's over."
I had no idea he was religious and obviously delighted we both had survived this exercise. Now for the landing. Aces have no problems with their landings, oh yes they do, we hit the ground like a ton of you know what. So what happened to the beautiful forgiving aircraft I once had so much respect for. The Chipmunk is, without doubt, a wonderful machine in the air but when coming in contact with the planet things change slightly. After completing God knows how many circuits the great day for my solo flight was close.

As a 56 Squadron ATC civilian instructor I was the guest of the aircrew of 56 Squadron at R.A.F Wattisham when on a summer camp. I had the opportunity to witness the then famous "Firebirds" aerobatic team at practice flying their stunningly decorated Lightnings. During this visit I was presented with a second-hand headset, mask, white kid gloves and a new red and white chequered scarf by the squadron junior pilot a good luck gift. I was now ready to meet the challenge of my solo flight, fully kited.

Having satisfied my instructor and our C.F.I. I was not going to kill myself I completed my first solo flight with a landing that resembled a cat pissing on silk. A proud moment for all aviation enthusiasts. The following day became even more exciting having to complete my second solo check-out. Arriving at the club house I met Tiny walking towards me.
"Morning Tiny, What's for me today?" I asked.
"Get lost." He replied and marched on.
BINGO, I'm free. Nobody in the office so I signed myself out, checked the Chipmunk over, wings, fuselage, precise detail was paid to this exercise before every flight, let's go. It was a beautiful sunny day, mid-week days at Biggin were very quiet with few movements, I taxied to 23 grass applying full throttle when in no time I was back in the air passing over the wire fence at the end of the runway, my mind reflecting on my Meteor flight with Flying Officer Ian Smith. Was they're a little boy looking up through the fence eyes full of envy. 500 Feet turn right heading 010, 65 knots still climbing, 1500 feet level out, speed 90 knots trim out. Just south of the River Thames I recognised Brands Hatch, the famous race circuit then I had

that feeling I was about to do something very stupid. 360 turn, clear sky, wings level, full throttle nose down 120 knots on the clock, balls in the centre, pull back, I'm upside-down, check wings, still there, handy I thought, pull out, wing level, 360 turn, great no Hun and clear of all danger. YIPPEE. At last total freedom. Right I'm ready for my first ground attack mission and what better place to destroy but my council tip. Heading 260, target in sight. Full throttle nose down, balls in the centre, 120 knots over she goes into a clean loop followed by several aileron turns on the way down allowing me to attack at a different angle pulling up and completing another loop. Council tip destroyed, heading 150, back to Biggin.

Photo: © Pilots Pals

G-AOTG & Myself Biggin Hill 1963

Flying back To Biggin Hill I felt pleased with my flying, satisfied I had the ability to perform basic aerobatics but also understanding I had much more to learn from my instructors. I had not yet stalled, spun or even had any tuition in cross county flying. Lots to look forward to. Landing back on 23 grass I slowly taxied the aircraft to the south east apron. On completing the closing down procedure and removing my headset I slide the canopy back only to be met by the loudest request I had experienced. Tiny obviously wanted my attention

"MERCHANT WHERE THE BLOODY 'ELL HAVE YOU BEEN. GET IN 'ERE."

I remembered my ATC training, only give your name, rank and number. In other words say as little as possible should your nose tells you, "you're in it". Tiny was banging his head on the club wall while very slowly saying

"When-I-told-you-to-get-lost-I-didn't-mean-get-lost"

"Tiny I didn't get lost, I'm back" I replied.

"I know your bloody well back, where the bloody 'ell have you been?"

"Around." I replied trying so very hard not to giggle.

The rest of his intense verbal seem to disappear as I realised that I was in Sqn. Ldr "Bob" Eeles old office, on the very spot I had saluted my farewell to 615 back in 1957. What would Bob have done if I had been under his command. Because of my stupidity was this to be a repeat of my past.

"Are you listening to me Merchant." Tiny screamed.

"Ah yes Tiny, I'm so sorry to have placed you in this situation." I said, thinking, *Jesus we haven't got to the aerobatics yet.*

"I can't stand you bleeding aces, go get a cuppa tea.". He shouted.

I moved very quickly from the office straight to the greasy spoon, our place for refreshment. Sipping at the hot tea my thoughts were, I must get away with this somehow, the thought of loosing my flying was unbearable. Did Tiny know what I had been up to, did he send another aircraft after me as was the practice in those days for lost student pilots. Was I spotted by the anti aviation personnel that seem to breed so rapidly in the South East of England. I spent sometime, again, reflecting on my days with 615, those wonderful days ended in disaster. Suddenly Tiny walked in, put his face to mine with teeth rattling, I thought he was going to kiss me goodbye instead he said.

"The tea was for me, Pillock!"

No more was said. I had been very stupid to put myself and my aircraft in the situation that could have proved so dangerous. I left the "Bump" that day so excited, proud and a lot wiser knowing how very lucky I had been not to have been involved in an unexpected stall or spin of which I had zero experience.

The Surrey and Kent Flying Club plus the social club, their three Chipmunks G-APPK, G-AOTG, G-ATTS were now a part of my life. So, I had lost the Meteors together with the spirit of the R.Aux.A.F. but I was back on Biggin Hill in the same building as my old Squadron, learning to fly. I continued my Private Pilots Course flying to a small strip in Kent called Headcorn. We could only practice forced landings there due to runway 29/11 not being completed. On my first approach, keeping my eye on a flock of sheep happily munching away at the far end, I failed to see the many surveying poles placed on the proposed runway and I was forced to abandon my touch and go. My instructor agreed it was close. All student pilots had to complete the syllabus as laid down by the (Committee Against Aviation.)

Navigation exercises provided the opportunity to visit various airfields. My first dual cross country, apart from Headcorn, was an airfield North of Biggin Hill called Stapleford. After completing the necessary paper work, heading, estimated time etc., off I went with all the confidence of a true aviator, my instructor not saying a word. Taxiing, power and control checks all came second nature to me. The take off was from 23 grass climbing out of the circuit in a northerly direction until I was bang on track, over the River Thames into the unfamiliar flat territory of Essex. Stapleford should be on the nose any minute, two, three, four. Suddenly I spotted two beautiful hard runways, okay I was a little out on my estimated time but we had arrived. Cutting the power to start my descent, suddenly my instructor said

"And what are going to do now."

"Err land." I replied, a little hesitant thinking why would Charlie in the back ask such a question.

"What airfield is that." He asked.

"Stapleford." I answered.

"I have control, now look again." He shouted.

A small dose of panic arrived unexpectedly, a view of an airfield similar to that of Biggin Hill left me speechless.

"That is North Weald, now navigate to Stapleford, you have control."
He said.

Looking at my map again I saw that I had more or less flown over the grass strip of Stapleford. Oh don't you feel a plonker when you purport to be a laid back ace and then prove you are a potential hazard to all and sundry who share the same bit of blue. I simply hadn't studied my map well enough before the flight. Another lesson learned.

Continuing the P.P.L. course the big day arrived for my G.F.T. (General Flying Test). Tiny, my C.F.I., would put me through hell, I knew it but the more he asked of me the more I loved it. The memory of that test will stay with me all my life completing every detail to his satisfactory grunt. My confidence was running like Guinness at a Irish wedding.

Flying meant so much to me and it was one thing in my puny life that wasn't going to have failed written on it although I did have a small problem when Tiny gave me an engine failure in the circuit on our return from this test. I managed to put the aircraft on the numbers of 29 and as far as I was concerned a satisfactory ending to this flight. I taxied the chipmunk very slowly back to parking area waiting comments from Tiny but, not a word from him. Completing the closing down procedure we both walked to the office, still no word. I could not stand the prolonged agony of his silence.

"Well Tiny, how did I do." I asked.

"Lucky." He replied.

After my debriefing Tiny congratulated me on what he called a touch and go situation.

"You won't kill yourself will you Merchant." He said.

"Not today Tiny." I replied smiling.

Thanks to my previous ATC. flights I had completed the 30 hour P.P.L. course in 28 hours 45 minutes.

"What shall I do with the 1 hour 15 minutes left to complete my course Tiny?" I asked.

Tiny looked at me for a few seconds rattled his false teeth followed by a wink and said

"Get lost Merchant."

I'll take Papa Kilo, how is she for fuel." I said.

"CHECK THE BLOODY THING YOURSELF, DO YOU WANT ME TO WIPE YOUR NOSE." He screamed.

I signed myself out grabbed my flying helmet.

"Authorise my flight Tiny." I said trying so hard not to show my rushed enthusiasm to get back in the air. This last flight for my P.P.L was to be a cross county exercise. I can be perfectly honest the only straight lines I flew on that exercise were the take-off and landing. The long hours working 7 days a week, the continuous yearning to be a part of aviation finally rewarded all my efforts and dreams, not forgetting other pilots who gave me their time, inspiration and encouragement.

Photo: © Gordon Ankorn

G-APTS Chipmunk over the old 615 Squadron's hangar

The first Biggin Hill Air Fair 1963

This was the start of what became a welcome annual event, particularly for those in the South East of England; always provided the visitors had no objection to waiting in their cars for sometime both on arrival and departure.

Photo: Via Dan Graham

56 Squadron R.A.F. "The Firebirds"

9 Lightning's from 56 Squadron's aerobatic team that visited Biggin Hill air shows during the early 60's. The squadron C.O was Sqn .Ldr. D Seward who I had the pleasure of meeting during the 56 A.T.C. Squadron summer camp   at R.A.F. Wattisham. This must have been the most expensive aerobatic team in aviation history.

Photo: Via Air Touring

South East Apron
The new dwellings are the extension to Hawthorn Avenue complete 1980

Photos: © Norman Rivett North West view

1/ Wireless Road - Industrial Estate. 2/ Churchill Way 3/ Crossly Close . The first M.o.D. Quarters built 1917. 4/ Koonowla Close with Dowding Road. 5/ Hawthorne Avenue. 6/Jail Lane. 7/ Runway 11/29. 8/ Atcost Ltd. Hangar.

East view

1/ Runway 11/29. 2/ South East Apron. 3/Atcost Ltd. 4/ Alouette F.C. 5/ 600 Squadron Flying Group. 6/ Churchill Way. 7/ Surrey & Kent Club House.

South West View of South East Area

The Company Alcost Ltd. were responsible for building the first civil hangar. This project was for Bernie Fell and was completed during 1963. It is the light coloured hanger top right of this photograph.

1963 South East apron

600 Squadron's Tiger G-AOES before its sale to County Flying Club. The D.H Mosquito was one of the batch of 4 used in the epic film "633 Squadron" in 1962. Note the old control tower . I have seen red flares come out of the tower that would shame November 5th. Photos: © Norman Rivett

1963

The Flairavia Flying Club used the Bolkow Junior BO 208A -1 for their PPL courses with a great deal of success. I saw Ian Dezial (Doc) land this machine on 29 with the canopy open. It opened from the leading edge but the locking system failed. Such was the force and speed of the canopy being forced back it left a neat crease in the fuselage. I saw Ian a couple of hours later and he still had tears in his eyes.

Photos: © Norman Rivett

Surrey & Kent's G-AOTG.

Two of my favourite things. The Chipmunk and the Surrey & Kent Club bar..

Photo: © Norman Rivett

Flairavia's Champion Tri- Traveler G-APYT

This ski modification was the work of David Quirk, the late John George and David Porter, the principal of Flairavia, who drew up the plans using photos of light aircraft on skis. The late Bill Webb also made a few suggestions. Dexion was purchased from Orpington and the skis from a furniture manufacture located in North London. They were glad of the work as the country was then at a stand still because of more than 8 weeks of heavy snow. Vendair provided the rubber straps. The ARB gave the club the okay with pilot only restrictions. Several flights were made over the following days; David Porter reported the aircraft handled well in the air and found the skis gave it a better rate of climb. However, manoeuvring on the ground was more difficult as there was no form of braking and the rudder had little effect on maintaining a straight line except when under full power and take off. Alas braking was to be the downfall, when taxiing back to the hangar after a day flying the nose ski passed over an area free of snow whereupon the ski locked on the ground causing the nose leg to bend allowing the prop to clip the ground. Flairavia received a bit of jovial criticism and praise from many quarters for their efforts and determination to get the club flying in the most appalling weather.

Around the middle of 2000 this aircraft was converted to a tail dragger operating from Watchford Farm, Devon.

Chapter Seven

Whilst employed by W.F. Stanley, where I was a member of the Amalgamated Engineering Union, I was approached by my co-workers to take up the vacant position of shop steward. To be truthful I hated all unions classing them as un-British. Nevertheless I accepted the post hoping I would be able to bring the role of the unions into the 20th century. My concept that we should limit our meetings to the needs of our fellow worker and not to the more general concerns of the branch and district rules and regulations, immediately this brought me into bitter conflict with other shop stewards.

When attending my first branch meeting at Eltham Well Hall, South East London, I was able to put forward my views on modernising the thinking of our union by allowing each company union to resolve local disagreements and avoid bringing in branch, or district officials, who had little idea of the nature of local problems. The welfare of the individual member was irrelevant to both the branch and district levels of Union activity so there was little point involving them. To me these people were a waste of time. In my view the Stewards at individual factories should be empowered to deal directly with their own management. Underpinning my policy was the personal dictum that if you don't like your job for any reason move on. Why stay in a job that makes you unhappy when there was a chance the move could result in an improved salary. After delivering my view I was applauded by the other stewards who shook my hand and referred to me as "Brother." Though not sure that I warmed to the fraternal remark I accepted their appreciation.

I was then asked by the branch chairman to attend the next district meeting in London to further advance my education in union matters. At that meeting the first item on the agenda was the cancellation, due to the lack of funds, of the annual coach trip for retired members. I objected to this and requested that the union should scrutinise other items of expenditure with a view of making the day trip a priority; it went very quiet. I stressed my point stating that if it was not for the senior members the union would not exist. I was asked to sit down and did so.

On my return to work at W. F. Stanley I was summoned to the office of the chief steward and told I had been dismissed from the union. The chief stated.
   "I've never heard of anyone being sacked from the union before, you're the first."
I was pleased as punch to have such a unique recognition.

Chapter 8

To have achieved a life's ambition, plus the bonus of making so many new friends all sharing a common interest, life had become very exciting. All seemed endless fun enjoying the 'joie de vivre' that came so naturally from most of the members. At that time I believed I had a charmed life, but on reflection I realised I had worked long and hard to reach this goal. The catalyst was Biggin Hill, the people provided the ingredients to complete the formula. 1964 was a sad year for both me and Biggin Hill. Bromley Council absorbed Orpington due to boundary changes. Things were about to deteriorate.

Joseph J. Merchant 1997

Having successfully completed my Private Pilots Licence I purchased a Durkopp Diana 200 cc scooter from my dear sister, Rosemary, this unfortunately, had similarities to the horse in Wiltshire, I continued to fall off. It was time to upgrade my transport to 4 wheels more befitting the image of a young private pilot. Finding a beautiful one-year-old modified Mini on Bernie Eccleston's forecourt in Bexleyheath was a bit of luck, bearing in mind this was before the Mini Cooper. To get one already beefed-up was not easy; with twin Webber carburettors, shaved head and modified exhaust, sounds like a recent girlfriend. Registration 818 DLX. I bet most people remember their first car registration. My journeys to Biggin Hill became both more frequent and more comfortable arriving at the flying club in a shirt and tie rather than the all weather outfit of a motorcyclist. I had all I wanted, comfort, not just for me but for my dear Mother. No more lugging shopping from Well Hall for her, this was now my duty and pleasure for she suffered with a serious heart condition. I enjoyed cleaning and helping with the weekly washing. Dad had purchased a John Bloom twin tub washer-spinner machine to replace the dolly tub and posser method we had used for many years. Despite all our efforts we lost this wonderful, funny, loving Mother on the 13th May 1964. The pain of such a loss returned ten fold and I found it extremely difficult to cope with the emotional strain. Anger welled up and showed in many ways; I was not at all positive to my closest friends. I stayed away from Biggin Hill, why I don't know. Would this deep wound ever heal I asked myself?. I turned to my local church seeking help from our vicar praying he could help me ease the pain. After a short time listening to him I found a new inner strength and understanding in his every word. His final statement has echoed throughout my life.

"Time will heal the wound."

How right he was.

Continuing with my civilian instructor duty with the ATC placed me in a position of responsibility for all the young cadets, a duty of which I was very proud. To encourage the members of our squadron I offered a reward of 30 minutes flying in the Chipmunk to the best cadet of each month during the summer. This was a great success and it gave me the opportunity to give them some of what I had experienced with Royal Air Force over my years as a cadet. One Friday evening, a parade night, when searching my car for something or other I was startled by a car horn. I turned around to be confronted by the grinning face of Tony Wilcox, now Flying Officer Wilcox

Royal Air Force. Tony explained he was on leave for a short time and that this visit would be his only opportunity to catch up with his old friends at 56. This unplanned evening gave Tony time to tell of his life in the R.A.F. from training to his then position with 208 Squadron flying an FGA9 Hunter in Aden. The rest of that evening turned into one of laughter and consuming several pints of Guinness, our favourite brew. It was as if time had stood still, the old days back again but as always our evening was to end with slightly blurred farewells with the local police asking us to move on due to the high level of laughter.

"Bye mate, until the next time." I said.

However, there would never be a next time. Back in Aden on 30th June 1964, two Hunters of 208 Squadron had a mid-air collision during a practice ground attack strike. Flying Officer Tony Wilcox died instantly. I cried openly and unashamedly.

I was courting a young lady Officer of the Girls Venture Corps whose ambition was to obtain her pilots licence; winning the annual Flying Scholarship awarded to one lady within the corps, could make this possible. During a planned visit to Rochester Airport for one of her test flights I failed to recognise a road change in the city centre causing chaos in the one way system. Who should be waiting for such an event but a police motorcyclist who followed me and eventually waved me down to stop. There's little old me Mr. Nobody trying to impress this beautiful young lady, smart car, holder of a pilots licence with a few bob in my pocket. Jesus, I had a big problem. Unbeknown to this lady I had no road tax and four Kojak tyres, a certain *nick*. Before the police officer could dismount his machine I was out of the car approaching the officer at speed immediately apologising for the chaos I had caused.

"Where are you going?" Asked the officer.

"I'm trying to find Rochester Airport." I replied.

"Oh, your a parachutist are you?" He asked.

"No sir I am a pilot" I replied in a superior tone.

The noise that came from his riding boots reminded me of a Officer from the Third Reich greeting Hitler. Standing to attention the officer gave me clear instructions to our destination completing this amazing performance by saluting me fare-well and

"Safe journey Sir."

Loved it.

Wiping the beads of sweat form my brow I returned to the car full of confidence and panache. I had pulled the wool over this gentleman's eyes with bullshit without trying. This was a very valuable lesson that I would apply to my life in many ways, learning the skill of extracting the best out of a bad situation would be aided by the many characters I was to meet during my wonderful days at Biggin Hill. This education was to win over your opponent ensuring all parties benefited from this skill. The Police officer was happy, he had met a real pilot.

Photo: © Derek Bishop

Biggin Hill Flying Club 1964

Biggin Hill Flying Club was situated next to 600 Squadron Flying Group on the South East area. Pictured left to right above are: David Milstead - Eric Hill, Instructor - Dennis Andrews - Norman Rice - Goerge Stewart, Chairman The event a wine gathering flight to Berck-sur-Mer on the 10th July. The Auster J/5 Aiglet G-AMTD crashed attempting an overshoot at Hayrich Farm, Devon 7th August 1993. The wings were seen in a Leicester hanger during 2009.

BHFC also operated Auster J/5 Aiglet G-AOEZ that crashed near Sandown, Isle of White 30th July 1966 .

The Surrey & Kent fleet 1964   Photos: © Norman Rivett

A very wet and dismal day at Biggin Hill. Flying nil an ideal time for a photo shoot. The S & K Club House can be seen in the background. No toilets, men left, girls right.

Air Fair 1964

The 1964 Air Fair was a four day event with the U.S.A.F. Providing a C-124 Globemaster II. On promotional tour a Sud-Aviation Gardan GY80 G-ASJY.

Caledonian Douglas DC-7 G-AOIE

The majority of the population of the UK had not seen a commercial aircraft this close before, package tours were still in their early days. The thousands of visitors who queued for sometime to view the interior amazed me.

Photos: © Norman Rivett

Bristol B.170 Freighter

I was to experience a flight in this type the following year crossing the English Channel. The dentist replaced all my missing filings on my return.

Chapter Eight

I was to marry my girlfriend Janice on 24th December 1964 and planned to spend our honeymoon in Paris. I borrowed £100.00 from Dad to cover the cost. Our great day arrived and soon we were due to board our flight to France. However, remember the old saying "If you have time to spare go by air" 26 hours later we arrived in Paris having spent one hell of a night in a bar with half the Belgium Navy crossing the English Channel by ferry. Flying cancelled due to bad weather. The strange experience of spending our first night on honeymoon in the ship's bar with these chaps has given me a very high regard for the Belgium people. Not one of those gentleman tried to get me in bed that night. This admiration continued throughout my life, flying the Belgium flag in the Pilots Pals Bar with a great deal of pride. The best people, beer, food and the best flying club in NATO. The Belgium Air Force have attended the Biggin Hill air show for many year, initially they displayed 'Les Manchots' - a pair of formation Stampe SV4's.Les. Both pilots became great admirers of one of the Flairavia bar staff, Daphne Harris.

Janice, my wife, won the flying scholarship and despite her height and a previous illness she wanted to complete her training on the Chipmunk. I made a wooden extension seat for the Chipmunk allowing Janice to reach the rudder pedals and not interfere with the full movement of the control column. A few flights with me proved Janice had the courage and ability to handle the aircraft.

Surrey & Kent Flying Club with its three Chipmunks was wonderful but the members did lack the fun loving comradeship I yearned for. Suddenly I was informed by our C.F.I. that Papa Kilo, then my favourite aircraft, was not available as it was on loan to 600 Squadron Flying Group. I also learned that flying with 600 was cheaper for the same aircraft. Wasting no time I applied for membership; this was greeted with enthusiasm. I was also hoping to meet some of the old 615 crew but to my disappointment not one of the air or ground crew had continued their association with Biggin Hill. Another flying club yet another check flight with a well know character by the name of David Quirk. Later he was to form a partnership with another instructor Paul Shires, the new club becoming QS Aviation. They made a great team where the fun was endless if not sometimes a little boisterous. I had known David to be a competent pilot who won the respect of all that flew with him so my check-out was to be challenging due to his very high standard. Taxiing out and run up checks complete, you looked at other aircraft to see the runway in use. I have known three in use at one time that I can only explain as very exiting with so many red flares in the sky you would think it a Spanish festival. Arriving at 23 grass I had checked that no other aircraft were on finals, began applying full power at a steady rate adjusting for swing with the rudder, then more rudder.

"JESUS" Shouted David.

I had full right rudder on with the stick between the private parts, with power off we had completed a full 180°. Thanks to the long wet grass the aircraft stayed on all three points with no damage. After closing down David inspected the left hand undercarriage confirming that the left hand brake had locked on, the aircraft was only capable of turning in a circle. This turned into an epic with club members arriving from every bunny hole on Biggin giving their opinion on the cause and necessary remedy.

"Push it back." "Kick it." "Pull if forward." cried the members.

These chaps had obviously been to technical school.

"Sod it, the bar's open, who's for a beer." Said one of the team.

Surrey & Kent engineers collected the Chipmunk, I followed the members ending up at the Flairavia's bar giving me the opportunity to get to know the pilots of 600 Squadron. Some were ex Royal Auxiliary, others from clubs wishing to fly Chipmunks. By the end of the day I knew I had found what was missing, the comradeship, the hail fellow well met types that I had known so well with 615 Squadron.

Having checked out satisfactorily with my new club I was to continue meeting all the other members, not all whom flew. Some members were happy to continue flying dual on their student pilots licence having no wish to complete the course, others were members solely for the social side, happy just being in the environment of Biggin Hill and the people. Although the cost of 600 squadron's Chipmunk was the cheapest on the airfield at that time, it was one of the most expensive trainers to operate. It was no surprise to me that so many student pilots wanted to train on this machine, some like me, having the experience with the ATC air experience flights. The cost seemed secondary having once flown this great little aircraft.

I continued working at W. F. Stanley, happy and contented with the increase of my wages, unhappy with the management of whom were determined to destroy the company by demoralising the employees with their stupidity. My outspoken approached upset the directors but I was promoted to the planning office. Now, I thought, I could be more active in production by applying my knowledge to the products and their many problems. What you think you can do and what you can actually achieve are two different things. My war with the management escalated creating even more frustration.

Back at Biggin Hill 600 Squadron Flying Group was the remains of the old 600 Squadron R.Aux.A.F. disbanded in 1957 and for whatever reason seemed to attract humorous people not connected with the R.A.F. There was no doubting that the club was a cheerful, pleasant environment for all who had a passion for aviation and made welcome by all members. I felt there was a small barrier among some of the ex R.Aux.A.F. types but they were out numbered by non service members and all seemed to operate satisfactorily from a shed known as the club house on the South East area of Biggin. The club's instructors were a great bunch, Steven Hay, one of the assistant instructors, a handsome man, well-spoken who carried his pet goat in the back of his Morris Minor Convertible. Shopping in the village with him was an experience you would not wish to miss. The reaction and screams that came from old and young ladies coming out of the shops with their bags full of goodies. Did you know a goat doesn't speak English so there's little point in shouting at it. John Chester another assistant instructor, handsome man who gave all his students confidence and all the time they required. Mike Townsend, another great guy. The C.F.I. was an ex 600 Squadron Meteor pilot, unfortunately not my cup of tea. The members were a very mixed bunch from bus driver, Harry Groves, call sign "Ding Ding"; Ron Tate sales chap, call sign "Wonlumportwo", he preferred tea to beer. Tony Ansell call sign "The Misguided Muscle"due to his academic achieve-ments and his place of employment, bit hush hush. Dennis Andrews a very keen type could make friends with almost anyone. Harry Lindup, Derek Sheffield a printing ink salesman, the best storyteller we had. Ron Riddock, bit too serious for me but he did enjoy his flying. Joe Keyte, Harry Batton and L.A.C. Gwyn Russell R.A.F. stationed at A&AEE, Boscombe Down, he was one of my favourite people and I loved him like a Brother having a tremendous personality, we flew together on many occasions. Gene O'Leerie who insisted using those old throat mikes. Trying to understand his deep voice was like communicating inside a cement mixer full of empty beer cans and marbles.

I was not satisfied with my own flying, I was safe but not 100% happy. when flying with an old friend in the Chipmunk, John Twydell, an ex R.A.F. Pilot, he suggested I fly the Tiger Moth for few hours.
"That should sort you out." He said laughing.

I joined the County Flying Club to fly their Tiger Moths and to meet with Bob Needham, one of their assistant instructors. After one hour 45 minutes I went solo in G-AOBO feeling very happy with this old lady. To increase my flying hours with the view of obtaining my assistant instructors rating I flew the Turbulent, it was the cheapest way to increase ones hours, unfortunately I was bored out of my mind sitting in this toy, I have always said you need two of this type of aircraft. One for each foot, So back to the Tiger Moth enjoying the spirit of the County Flying Club and its members. On one flight I flew with an old ATC friend Pete Vickery who commented on landing

"Did you see that cyclist as we went over that hedge.".

"No." I replied

"Well if he had his mouth open any wider we would have gone straight down it." He said laughing.

Having completed 5 hours solo in the Tiger I returned to the Chipmunk since it was now winter. Winter in the open cockpit of a Tiger is not a very good experience; it leaves you numb in every joint.

Mick Ronayne
Chief Flying Instructor, County Flying Club 1962 - 1970

South East Camp Biggin Hill

G-ANKB one of the four Tigers operated by the County Flying Club . Seen in this shot is Mick Ronayne demonstrating effects of controls to a few of his new members. The chap with a beard and glasses is Bob Needham now retired living in Australia painting aviation scenes from his past. . County's other Tigers were G-AOES. G-APFU. G-AOBO. The white building in the background was the South London Aero Club.

Image of Biggin Hill

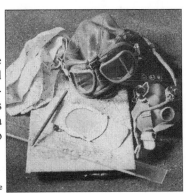

Mick Ronayne gave me this image saying one day it should be published to portray the spirit of Biggin Hill during the 60's. I am pleased knowing his wish has come to fruition, he was a man admired by all his team and too his students.

Photos: Via Mick Ronayne

Turbulent's were an inexpensive flying hour builder, I found them boring due to the limited stress level. Biggin lost G-APKZ attempting aerobatic manoeuvres 6/12/60

The Turbulent Formation Team based at Headcorn are great fun worthy of a visit to their home in Kent.

G-ARCZ was written off 1/6/84

Me having fun 16/10/65

Photo: © Pilots Pals

de Havilland D.H 82A Tiger Moth
By
Bob Needham

Bob Needham proved his ability as a flyer and now in semi retirement in Australia he produces watercolour scenes of his memories of Croydon and Biggin Hill. The above painting of Tiger Moth G-AIDB from the Pioneer Flying Group , Croydon Airport December 1956, captures the typically bad weather of a 1950's English winter. My last instructor at S & K, Roger Bailey, sent himself solo in this aircraft, another hero to my list .

"Buttocks Boarder"
By
Bob Needham

Clive was odd, very decidedly odd. One could almost say he was close to being that oddest of all things - an English Eccentric. He had a laugh which I always thought sounded something like a bark or, perhaps , a cough. A sort of booming "HUT HUT HUT" sound. Even more arrestingly it was about the equivalent of a Force 10 on the Beaufort scale, as any flying instructor will tell you, force 10 is a storm and easily recognised as such since trees start to be uprooted and considerable structural damage is done in one's immediate vicinity. In short his laugh was seriously loud. Sometimes when laughing, his face though beet red would remain quite impassive and on first meeting with Clive this could be quite unnerving to say the least. All this, together with a set of eyebrows that made Anthony Quinn's luxurious growths pale into miserable insignificance would, in most other company, have made him a particularly remarkable character. However in juxta position with all of the other remarkable characters of the 1960's Biggin Hill he passed in as averagely normal.

Clive also had a passion for words which, no pun intended, bordered on the bizarre. Not so much the meaning of words but more the sounds that they might make. Having fastened on to a new word he could be heard and seen wandering around the aerodrome at all hours repeating the word in as many different permutations as it's component syllables would allow. He would then contrive to introduce the word into the conversation at every opportunity.
This produced some very odd pronunciations of perfectly normal English words being used in not always appropriate contexts. Although all this was a source of amusement for Clive it was often disconcerting for passing strangers.

For some days before our crash on the 1st March 1966, in the County Flying Club's Auster Xray Pa-pah, Clive had been conducting linguistic experimentation with the word buttocks. Butt-ocks, but-tocks, boo-ttocks, you know; that sort of thing. Anyway we were on the homeward leg of a navex to Staplford and Ipswich and battling with that dirty yellow smog that was so common to the east of London in those days. Suddenly, as Mrs. Robinson would have it, we could hear - "The sound of silence". My immediate response was the classic "shit the engine's stopped" Clive's rejoinder of "BUT-tocks, it has too" was less classic I felt, but equally ineffective in restoring the noise. Realising that neither of these responses seemed materially to improve our situation I started to pump the throttle. Well, as even the most inexperienced of pilots knows, this action is guaranteed to contribute absolutely nothing and is therefore not particularly recommended. However this is not the place to dredge through the minutia of the whole sorry fiasco. Suffice to say that the national grid, a farm house and a hedge were all kaleidoscopically and memorably compressed into the next few minutes. Finally the whole box of dice terminated with Clive and me saturated in petrol, hanging upside down and trapped inside an inverted wreck of an aeroplane in a boggy field somewhere in darkest Essex.

Our exit from the aeroplane is yet another story, but the saga rolled on and we found ourselves explaining our predicament in the midst to the local farmer person, ambulance persons, assorted passing yokel persons and the local constabulary person. The usual, "are you the owner of this ere hairplane sir" routine was patiently endured; after which the locals released us and we ignominiously made our way, by public transport, back south of the river and hence to civilization.

Looking back now I believe Clive and I were suffering from some sort of delayed reaction, since on our journey home we seemed to think that every single thing that was said by either of us was uproariously, side splitting, funny. Our progress was marked by Clive "hut hut hutting" at full volume, much misuse of the word buttocks and me rolling around all over the place clutching my sides. This, together with the fact that we were both covered from head to toe in good solid Essex mud and smelling to high heaven of Avgas, ensured that the pair of us travelled back to the protective sanctuary of Biggin Hill in perfect isolation; even though it was the height of the rush hour!. Like most people that knew him, I had always thought of Clive as "Eyebrows Boarder". For ever after that, I thought of him by no other name.

16th December 2005
Wauchope
NSW
Australia

Chapter Eight

As Bob Needham has written, Biggin Hill in the 60's seemed to breed characters who could amuse an entire airport. If things were quiet then the pilots and students created their own amusements in a variety of ways , not just flying. We had a very large facility, an airport, that could provide endless opportunities for enjoyment. The main runway, 03/21, had restrictions and use of this huge piece of concrete was only by permission of the management. However, after flying had finished the management could not be located and not wishing to waste the use of this one mile long facility, a car race could be organised, or rather disorganised. It became a free playground for all us young enthusiasts. Once when I had to leave the airport early and was driving onto the Main Road approaching the end of 21, a white sports car shot over the road and landed in the wooded valley. I had no time to help this budding aviator and drove on. Arriving back the following morning the vehicle had been recovered. The problem with racing on that runway it gave a false impression of where the end was located. The driver must have been an embarrassed novice for he, or she, was never to be heard or seen again.

Photo: © Pilots Pals

Girls Venture Corps Sergeant Lynne Newman swinging Tiger G-AOBO October 1965. Dressed for the weather, my wife Janice, in the front cockpit.

Flying Instructor Richard Elles

Richard Elles was one of the Biggin Hill instructors I was privileged to meet, who also became a lifelong friend. Richard devoted his life training pilots and was responsible for many enthusiasts obtaining their licence. G-APIP was operated by Vendair. Sadly this aircraft was lost with fatalities on 28th July 1963 at Hayes Common, Kent.

Photo: Via Pam Ellis

BIGGIN HILL COMMANDMENTS

1. Biggin Hill Airport is private property—Therefore thou shalt not trespass thereon.

2. Thou shalt park thy car neatly and not drive around the airfield—thus shall all pilots enjoy peace of mind.

3. Thou shalt walk in the paths of safety—on the outside of the perimeter track.

4. Thou shalt cast thine eyes to the skies, and obey the traffic lights, whether on foot or mechanised ass.

5. Thou shalt not touch thy neighbour's aircraft. It is more sacred to him than his motor car.

6. Thou shalt respect the grass and not litter it nor park thereon as if it were thine own garden.

7. Thou shalt not suffer thy children and dogs to stray into ways of danger.

8. Thou shalt obey the commands of Air Traffic Control as the true word—for they see all.

9. Thou shalt not enter the houses of the aircraft nor smoke nearby lest they become as the fiery furnace.

10. Thou shalt join a club—so that thou also may ascend unto the heavens.

I remember seeing these rules on the flying clubs notice boards and Dillow's restaurant (The Greasy Spoon). By Roy Taylor (Pipe) Airport Manager.

Chapter Eight

Chapter 9

I always felt as if the ghosts of the Battle of Britain were watching us with amusement and perhaps some degree of approval at our antics. For me they seemed to be ever present and I felt proud to be treading the same hallowed ground and flying in the same hallowed Kentish skies that they had only a short 15 years or so before us. The spirit, comradeship and characters at Biggin Hill were truly unbelievable.

Bob Needham 2009

Chapter Nine

My many hours experience flying the R.A.F. Chipmunks from the back seat coupled with experience on Tigers qualified me to fly our Chipmunk from the back seat. This allowed me to become one of the group check-out pilots that, in turn, gave me opportunities for free flying. Club rules required that all pilots not having flown for 30 days had to have a check-out. This was all the reason I needed to be at Biggin notwithstanding the fact my wife was having weekly instruction from John Chester and David Quirk. I would hang around waiting for every possible free trip. Unfortunately this was not a not a frequent occurrence since the group's pilots were real enthusiasts and flew almost every weekend. I pranced around in my flying suit in full view of the public who had free run of the South East apron; it gave me the opportunity to pick up the odd trip and to encourage others to join the group. I remember one occasion when I was approached by a very old lady.

"Are you a pilot son?" she asked.

"Yes madam." I replied respectfully.

"Long time since I've been called madam; can you take me up, I want to fly before I die."

It went through my mind when looking at this very old lady that both of these events could arrive at the same time. I then explained about the necessary documentation that would have to be completed before any flight plus the need for a donation to the club's coffee tin, She signed the blood chit, as we called it, and gave a very generous donation. Her signature had that 'pissed spider' look about it, this increased my concerns for this dear lady as her excitement was obviously at a peak. Our difficulty was getting her into the Chipmunk, it took two of our members to get her onto the wing and then lower her into the cockpit Strapping her in was my job, with suspenders and stocking being the order of the day. Head set on, she did look wonderfully silly. I jumped in the back, strapped myself in, then with headset on I had communication with my excited passenger. To ensure she had full confidence in me I took her through all the checks and then informed her I was about to push the starter. This I did, but there was only silence, not a burp from the engine. I informed her I would need a swing by another member. I'm sure that did not help her confidence. As I made my exit from the aircraft members started to walk towards me

"You sending her solo already Joe." Said one.

"Give us a swing, the bloody battery's dead." I replied.

"Just like your passenger eh Joe".

The negative comments were endless, and sapped my confidence to an all time low. The truth being, I wish my aged passenger had not asked me to fulfil her lifelong ambition, it was not going at all well. Back in the aircraft I shouted

"Switches off."

My assistant swinger started to pull through and shouted

"Contact."

Then yet more silence.

"Switches off!" Although several members volunteered to get it going, unfortunately not one of them was successful. Back in the club I gave her a refund from the coffee tin and promised to fly her the following weekend. However, I was never to see her again.

The number of new friends I made flying with both 600 and County had increased, one could not attend Biggin and be on one's own. One check-out I did was with a friend, Gene O' leery; it only needed a couple of circuits for me to know he did not like flying on his own, I too had known that feeling when flying the Turbulent. During our second circuit on the base leg, we were fast catching up with an Auster that had gone well past the turning for finals. I instructed Gene to turn for finals, thereby turning inside the Auster that appeared to be going cross-country. Gene turned 90° and lined to runway 11. All was going smoothly until both Gene and I realised we were now in formation with the Auster. My very loud instructions to Gene must have frightened him more than the sight of the formating Auster.

"Cut the power Gene, stick the nose down and land!".

This would show the Auster that we had taken the initiative to land first and thereby gain some distance between the two aircraft. The Auster flew over us and was forced to complete an extra circuit. That evening in the Flairavia bar I was introduced to the unfortunate student who I had forced to go-around . This extremely well spoken, polite young man who I took to be an accountant was not concerned with the potential danger but with the extra cost of seven shillings and six pence for his extended flying lesson This meeting was the first of many that subsequently developed into a lifelong friendship with Barry Wheeler, also known as "Scoop", the Aviation Journalist.

Biggin Hill circuits had increased in size over the years. I was taught to turn from down wind to base leg when the active runway came in line with the end of ones wing. Once on base leg reduce power and glide into finals. This practise was standard procedure and helpful should one's engine wish to take a rest or the propeller fell off. The circuit at Biggin was very busy, not that I was concerned about the number of aircraft in the air providing we were all going round the same way. On my first flight to Elstree I flew over head looking for the signals square to confirm which runway was in use and checked that the windsock agreed. On a previous occasion at Ipswich after looking at the signal square I failed to check the wind direction and then found I had a 90° crosswind on finals. I very nearly collided with one of their silly wooden red and white corner markers that showed the centre of the airfield. I soon made my views clear to the controlling staff whose reply was.

"Oh yes, I meant to change that this morning, sorry,"
Back to my Elstree flight. I landed safely and parked the Chipmunk close to the tower. Time for a cup of tea and pay my landing fee.

"Where you from sir?", Asked one of the staff.

"Biggin Hill", I replied.

"Oh the bee hive, bloody dangerous place Biggin Hill." Said another.
I immediately felt the hair on my neck bristle.

"And what is wrong with Biggin?" I asked.
The reply was instant,

"When our students choose to fly there we ensure that all documentation is complete and we have two Browning 303 machine-guns fitted to the aircraft to enable them to join the circuit. It's the only way to land there, shoot your way in."
The laughter was infectious and even I had to giggle knowing how busy Biggin could get particularly at weekend. My farewell comment was.

"Bye, happy landings."
After my cup of brew I was still laughing as I climbed into my Chipmunk to return home, Biggin Hill.

Flairavia Bar 1965

Left to right:
Barry Wheeler (Scoop)
Gwyn Russell (R.A.F.)
Bob Needham
Clive Boarder (Eyebrows)

Background
Tony Ansell
(The Misguided (Muscle)

Photo: © Pilots Pals

Since 1963 the Biggin Hill Air Fair, under the management of "Jock" Maitland, ,had proved successful. The 1965 show was exceptional with the arrival of a Lancaster from Australia. The Lancaster B.VII NX611 was one of a batch of surplus aircraft transferred to the French Government during 1952. Thanks to the determination of the Historical Aviation Society the French government agreed not only to donate an aircraft but have WU15 delivered by the French Navy (L'aeronaval) to Australia during 1963. After exhaustive fundraising and hard work G-ASXX, its new British registration, started its 12,000 miles journey home, landing at Biggin on the 13th May 1965. The comment heard from the pilot was *"I never want to get in that thing again."*. G-ASXX was test flown 14 times by Neil Williams during its stay at Biggin, however it was given notice to leave on 30th March 1967.

Biggin Hill Air Fair

Photo: © Bob Needham

G-ASXX touching down 13th May 1965

Photo: © Norman Rivett

1965 Biggin Hill Air Show saw the first UK public appearance of the Royal Air Force's new aerobatic team "The Red Arrows" . The name was formed from two previous successful R.A.F. Teams; "The Red Pelicans" and the "Black Arrows". The first Red Arrow team comprised of seven Folland Gnats. The team leader was the ex boss of the "Yellowjacks", Sqn. Ldr Lee Jones, Flt. Lt Ray Hanna was his number three. The latter, on promotion to Squadron Leader the following year, took over and was to lead the Reds for the another four years. It was under Ray Hanna's leadership in 1968 that the team increased to nine aircraft.

The Folland Gnat was the successor of the Folland Midge. I witnessed the prototype during my holiday in Highworth, Wiltshire during 1954. While cycling to the Vickers factory at South Marston, as I often did during holidays there, hoping to see some aircraft movements I saw a small blue jet aircraft in formation with a Lancaster. The small jet broke away, flying low over the Vickers factory, possible showing off. This unexpected display continued for sometime while the Lancaster circled the aerodrome. Then the unknown jet climbed away, suddenly turning very sharply to avoid a collision with the Lancaster. It would be sometime before I found out what aircraft it was but, the unmistakable colour and size had stayed in my young enthusiastic memory. It was the Folland Midge/Gnat on one of its early test flights from the Folland/Vickers Supermarine test aerodrome Chilbolton. NW of the Solent in Hampshire.

Biggin Hill Air Fair 1965 - South East Apron. Photo: © Norman Rivett

Once known as "The Travel Fair" the event had became very successful, thanks to "Jock" Maitland and his team. It was well supported by both civil and military aircraft. The black hangar was the H.Q. for 615 Squadron during the mid 50's, now Jet Aviation. The buildings in the right top corner are (i)Crossley Close, the first married quarters for the Royal Flying Corps 1917, and (ii) hangars once used for the storage of M.o.D. Green Goddess fire-engines and now industrial units, an extension to Wireless Road.

There was a difference of opinion regarding the use of the airfield for this show as Biggin Hill already had the annual "Battle of Britain" day during mid September. The moaners complained that it was disturbing the normal activities and the clubs were losing valuable income. As far as I was concerned it was all good fun with club members enjoying a free air show and meeting visiting crews, these without fail gave us the opportunity for a great party at the end of each day. During the show Neil Williams hit the ground rather hard while demonstrating the Stampe but survived this horrendous accident. I never had the pleasure of meeting Neil although he spent sometime at Biggin Hill. He was one of England's most talented pilots a former graduate at the of Empire Test Pilots School and 11 times British aerobatic champion. He was also an author of aviation books. I for one greatly admired his flying ability.

More new friends; Roy Sanders, call sign, P.1.G. due to both his appearance and eating habits. It was rumoured that he had his racing colours on his knife and fork. He was a wonderful person full of pranks and creating endless laughter. He was a professional chauffeur to the owner of a Rolls Royce in the entertainment world. Unfortunately he lost his employment when the owner, watching TV, saw his beloved car entered a stock car race. Douglas Gilbert VD & Scar, WC & Chain, call sign T.F.G. (That F'ing Gilbert). He was an Ex R.A.F. Fighter pilot, 1941 -1945, and son of a doctor. His father, understandably, had little time for his fun loving son and when informed by Douglas he was joining the R.A.F. to become a pilot replied

"Well you're no earthly use for anything else."

Well dressed, very well educated with a command of the English language that would shame Shakespeare. His entire appearance was that of a true English gentleman or possibly a tramp. The first time I met Douglas was in the Flairavia bar saying to me.

"Hello old boy, what's that?"

Placing a bamboo bird cage on the bar. I was somewhat taken back by the sight of a bamboo cage containing an aircraft instrument. The entire club burst into laughter.

Illustration by Pilots Pals

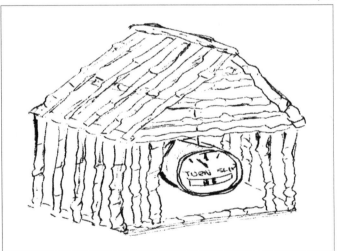

A caged gyro by Douglas Eastern Gilbert

Thus began a friendship that had all the ingredients of trouble. Robin Phillips, part time controller and private owner that used a Routemaster bus for his transport when he was tired of his London Taxi. He was yet another lifelong friend in the making. Rhys Perraton, another dedicated pilot who always reminded me of an American footballer, a tall handsome young man. David Perrin whose courage and ability would see him become the youngest member of the Rothmans' aerobatic team. Gavin Dix still flying to this day. Derek White one originator of the Alouette Flying Club in 1959, made his name training pilots in the U.S.A. I remember reading his adverts in the British aviation magazines stating the advantages of flying in the United States, his adverts always ending "Derek White, Ex Biggin Hill." That's how proud we all felt of our historic airfield. Derek McQoid, a very quiet and polite gentleman who made his name in imports.

One of the most likeable pilots I was to meet during this period was Ian Dalziel, call sign "Doc" due to his profession as a doctor. He had the most permanent infectious smile that could turn to laughter for any reason; greeting him was a pleasure. One of Biggin Hill's best known characters to this day is "Coby". Pilot and engineer, give him enough match sticks and he'll build you a Tiger Moth. He was always willing to help me all through the years I knew him. Mary Dillow was our provider of mugs of tea at the greasy spoon café situated on the South East apron. The café was the ex 615 Squadron armament room where I had spent many hours cleaning the unspent rounds of 20 mm ammunition . During the 60's it was the central meeting place before the many clubs each opening a bar to cater for their own pilots and staff. Christopher de Vere, owner of the Gemini G-AJWE and president of the Croydon Airport Society, was another fine gentleman with a wonderful enthusiasm for the preservation of all things aviation.

Another weekend

John Chester one of 600 Squadron assistant instructors and myself in a drinking mood after a flight.

The 600 club house was a shed come hotel, with a few hot and cold running women, situated next to the Avtech hangar on the South East area.

"The Greasy Spoon"

Mary Dillow's business supplied our mugs of tea and coffee. 8 years previous it was the armoury for 615 Squadron R.Aux.A.F. The strong smell of cleaning solvent being replaced by the aroma of eggs, bacon and beans.

South East Area

1965 shows the completion of the Officers quarters, Koonowla Close and Dowding Road. Koonowla House and the Army Mess had been demolished.

My dislike for politicians increased when the Government of the day under the Labour leader P.M. Wilson cancelled the TSR-2 project. All jigs and tooling had to be destroyed the day after the cancellation, the announcement made by the joker chancellor James Callaghan 6th April 1965. This joint project was awarded to Vickers and English Electric in 1959 as a replacement for the Canberra. The two companies became the British Aircraft Corporation in 1960. The project had its enemies, a prominent one being Lord Mountbatten. He took it on himself to go to Australia with 2 models, one of the TSR-2, the other of a Buccaneer, stating that you could have ten Buccaneers for the price of one TSR-2. No Australian orders were received for either of these by the British aviation industry. The future of the R.A.A.F rested with America. The Australian Government under P.M. Menzies ordered the F.111 in 1963, but it took ten years for the order to be delivered. It would appear that P. M. Wilson preferred to buy a replacement aircraft off the shelf for we then saw that the R.A.F. had agreed a purchase option on the F-111 prior to the cancellation of the TSR-2. Well done Harold you put so may of our aircraft engineers out of work only to cancel the options on the F-111 in January 1968. I have no idea how much this cancellation cost Britain. I do remember the chat on Biggin, people were looking forward to TSR-2 as potential British export product. With a high proportion of the research and development completed, many hours of prototype flying achieved the potential of the aircraft seemed certain. Of course we could all be wrong. TSR-2 the book by Tim McLelland, tells the whole story and is worth a read.

Looking back on our so called leaders we see many instances of errors of judgment and mistakes when it comes to investment in British industry. For example take Sir Frank Whittle and his team. Why on earth did it take so long for these idiots to see the future of gas turbines. Also the Schneider Trophy would not have been won for Great Britain had not Lady Lucy Houston donated £100,000. The Government of the day withdrew its support for the event when Sir Hugh Trenchard opined and I quote.
"Nothing of value in it." Moron.

As history has shown the private financial help from Lucy Houston gave Supermarine and Rolls Royce a good foundation for the Merlin engine that powered so many aircraft when England was on its knees. There were many nights when the members of Biggin Hill and I'm sure many other airfields discussed the failings of the morons that had control of our purse strings.

Gavin Dix & Mick Ronayne County Flying Club

Clive Boarder (Eyebrows) with G-AOBO during his P.P.L. training with County Flying Club 1966. The hangar in the background was the H.Q 600 Sqn. R.Au.A.F. who's Honorary Air Commodore was the Queen Mother.

Chapter 10

The summer of 1966 was in front of us leaving behind those cold winds from the North East that seem to penetrate our exposed airfield 600 feet above sea level. Those aroma's of Spring would sometimes return as early as February reminding me of my youth. I would drive to the airfield looking for snowdrops, new shoots of grass, early buds that took on a refreshing picture of new and longer days.

Joseph J. Merchant 2009

John Miles celebrating with Rex Nicholls Photo: © Norman Rivett

The 600 Squadron C.F.I., John Miles, won the Kings Cup Air Race in 1966 flying the Surrey and Kent Chipmunk G-APTS. I only flew with John on one occasion, in Hornet Moth G-AELO on a cross country from Biggin to Manston. During that visit I was invited to fly an R.A.F. Chipmunk, WP846, now N123BB U.S.A.. This provided me with a free 35 minute lesson in aerobatics by courtesy of H.M. Government. The return flight to Biggin in the Hornet Moth was uneventful; unfortunately I never had the opportunity to fly the old girl again. The privately owned (1937) Hornet Moth G-AELO, 8105, was impressed during 1940 becoming AW118. It returned to its original civilian registration in 1947, today this aircraft must be the pride and joy of its owner.

Hornet Moth G-AELO   Photo: © Norman Rivett

A new aviation venture, "The National Air Guard", was launched at Biggin Hill during the later part of 1966. The first and only unit in the UK, NAG No.1 Squadron was chaired by D. Hjelme-Lundberg, with cooperation from two acquaintances of mine, Derek White and Ron Turton. It was loosely structured on a military system with dark uniforms and ranks from Cadet to Commanding Officer. It closed during 1969 for what I could only imagine was financial reasons.

No. 1 Squadron N.A.G. 1966   Photo:© Barry Wheeler

The NAG Stinson G-AFVT was donated by Grundig (GB). This machine was sold to the USA in 1968. Their other aircraft were Cessna 175A G-ARCK and Aer Macchi AL60-B1 G-AXEZ, ditched off Yarmouth. 1969

Gene O' Leery returned to the club after several months absence from flying and requested I fly with him on a cross country check-out to Headcorn.

"No problem Gene."

I said, without really knowing if I could authorise such a trip. Gene completed his paper work and off we went on an enjoyable flight. Arriving over head Headcorn Gene asked if I would do the landing on the very short runway 03. Telegraph wires one end, a water ditch the other, meant one had to be sure of the final approach speed. After landing safely we both got out too stretch our legs when the unmistakable noise of rubber fighting tarmac drew our attention to a fast approaching cloud of dust containing a Ford and the grinning face of Derek Sheffield, a member of 600 who lived not too far from the end of the runway at Headcorn. After the dust cloud had settled we heard Derek's enthusiastic greeting;

"Hi Joe, hi Gene."

Quickly followed by

"Come on Joe let's go."

"Go where?"

I replied somewhat confused since Derek had no licence.

"Flying, I'll pay." he said.

I turned to Gene

"Is this okay with you Gene? We shouldn't be too long."

"Yes mate, you go enjoy yourself." He replied laughing.

Back in the Chipmunk, still very uncertain of my authority to pilot a non licensed student from the back seat. Derek took-off no problem, his airmanship was good but we had a lot more sky above us than we had beneath us.

"I'll show you my house."

he said while completing a ground attack manoeuvre. Christ I thought.

"Did you see it?"

He shouted with even more excitement.

"No."

I replied, immediately regretting my response and thinking I should have said yes as Derek lined up for another attack.

"Derek, best we get out of here the war has been over a few years now." I said

He chuckled and headed for runway 03 where he completed a good short landing. We said our farewells and Gene flew our Chipmunk back to Biggin landing on 23 grass as smooth as a babies undercarriage. Gene was a safe pilot but lacked a little confidence and perhaps didn't like flying on his own.

Chapter Ten

The following Saturday when approaching the club shed I was met by Derek walking towards me and speaking out the side of his mouth.

"Don't say a word about last week, we were never there, wife in club."
He then carried on walking. Later that day another member informed me that Derek was waiting for me in the Flairavia Bar. Great I thought he's buying me a beer for taking him flying last week.

"Ah, hi Joe."
If sound had a smell he sounded like the shit had hit the fan.

"Do you remember last week when we..."
I interrupted and said

"Hold it Derek, what's with the we bit."

"No, no listen, I'm in a bit of trouble over that flight last week and need your help. Should my wife ask you any questions regarding flying at Headcorn last week just say you were in Glasgow last Saturday."

"Why Glasgow?" I asked.

"Then bleeding Moscow, anywhere but Headcorn."
He said abruptly.

"Why all the fuss Derek?"
I was feeling a little concerned at this point.

"Well it's like this."
Then looking at me with those big puppy eyes he continued.

"Last weekend the Mother-in-law came for one of her long stays. To be perfectly honest I was bored out of my mind until I heard the sound of your Gipsy, it injected new life into me. Leaving home on the weakest pretext we all met up on the field. To cut this very long story short the first time we flew over the house the Mother-in-law was sitting in the garden, in her low cut summer dress, with our cat sitting on her lap. Problem one, the cat got airborne taking half her chest with it and ended up in the top of our apple tree. Problem two - After the second fly by it took more than three hours to get the bloody thing down and even then it couldn't walk due to the stiffness in its legs. As for the chest, that really did look sore. Now she's threatening me with the police, so not a word".

Boy, did I laugh and still do at the thought of that cat on top of the tree thinking he was in the best place. Well, he was if his needs were to see a Chipmunk head-on doing around 120 knots. Once Derek and his lady had left Biggin Hill that evening I felt free to tell the story of the Mother-in-law, cat and the tree in the Flairavia Bar much to the appreciation of the other members. After, nothing was ever said.

Illustration by Ben Holmes 2006

"Not me Mate"

I can imagine some pilots reading these stories could be justified with their criticism, these illegal activities were dangerous, foolish and most of all bloody great fun. I wish that I could do it all over again reliving those carefree days with those special people at Biggin Hill.

Photo: © Norman Rivett

Surrey & Kent's Chipmunks G-AOTG - G-APTS.

Hawker Sea Fury FB11 WJ288   Photo:© Barry Wheeler

This aircraft was on Biggin Hill for a short time before being transferred to Southend for the planned museum that opened its doors on the 26th May 1972 and closed on 27th March 1982. There followed an auction of their exhibits on 10th May 1983. Doug Arnold obtained the aircraft in 1988 and restored it to airworthy condition as G-SALY. It was shipped to the U.S.A. in 1991 and given the FAA registration N15S. . To think I could have bought four of these for less that £4,000 each at around the time Barry took this photograph, 1966.

My Good Friend

Carol, a lifelong friend from the late 50's, sunbathing outside 600's club house. I am ready for a day posing hoping to get some free flying from the many visitors that were free to roam the airfield, particularly at week-ends. As a private pilot it was illegal to fly for hire or reward. I therefore converted the flying hours into Guinness. 30 minutes flying = 6 pints. Note the B25 Mitchell parked outside Avtech's hangar and beyond the experimental Steel House built in the 60's   Photo: © Pilots Pals

Photo: © Norman Rivett

D H Chipmunk G-AOTY

600 Squadron's Chipmunk G-APPK, on hire from the Surrey and Kent Flying Club, was due for a maintenance check, possibly a new C of A leaving the members with no aircraft. Most the members had eyed the private Chipmunk TY enviously, longing to fly the immaculate machine that was parked on the east side of Biggin. One member of our group, still unknown to this day, approached the owner a Lugard Brains to negotiate the hire to the 600 Group. Negotiations completed @ £5.00 per hour wet we had the use of this almost new aircraft. I flew TY for 4 months not realising it upset our CFI John Miles as he had an interest in the hire from the Surrey & Kent Flying Club. Looking through my log book it appears I flew G-AOTG, G-APTS and, on its return to flying G-APPK. The club must have had the use of several aircraft, the first choice of any member would have been TY leaving the other members the use of which ever S & K aircraft was allocated to 600 Group.

At a party during this period I consumed a little too much while knowing I had to drive back home to Well Hall, my wife could fly but never drove so it fell to me to get us home. I reached Chislehurst Hill and realised I was in no fit state to continue our journey. Crawling from my Mini I lent against the car, eyes closed only to be greeted by a police officer.

"Good evening sir, not feeling well?" He asked.
"Far too much happiness officer." I replied.
"A short walk you'll feel better, good night sir.". A different planet then.

Experimental Flying Group June 1966 G-APRF
Members of E.F.G. Harvey Rollison, Graham Jackson & Keith Agate.

Harvey went onto commercial flying as a Skipper for B.A. Graham was a professional drummer. Keith was an engineering inspector working in New Addington, he was also a semi-professional trumpet player who sat in with many of the big names in the London jazz clubs. A great friend who hated live music during his drinking time, a problem for our club at party time that I could never understand.   .

The relationship among the 600 Flying Group and the Experimental Flying Group was a healthy one; albeit sometimes a little dangerous since both had a competitive spirit. I refer to the non aviation games that both clubs entered. Many of the E.F.G. members went onto become commercial pilots thanks to the dedication of Rex Nichols their Chief Flying Instructor and his team of assistant instructors. One E.F.G. instructor I had a run in with was a Peter Elliott a Captain for B.O.A.C. flying the VC10. telling him B.O.A.C. was a crap organisation. I had a thing about this airline buying the Boeing 707 and then advertising "Fly British." I bet those silly accountants at B.O.AC. wish they could turn the clock back and place orders for a further batch of VC10's. Time heals all and Peter and I went onto become good friends helping me with my ambitious club fly past.

B25 Mitchell 44-30861 " Moviemaker II" Photo: © Norman Rivett

Seen here parked on the Avtech hard standing this aircraft was imported from the USA as N9089Z and became G-BKXW. It was used for the filming of "The War Lover"and "633 Squadron"in the early 60's. I witnessed the deterioration of this aircraft over two years. Worst still, one Saturday morning I saw a chap removing the starboard wing with a giant cutter. With both wings literally torn off it was transferred to Southend by road for their museum. The last time I saw this aircraft was at North Weald in a most appalling state. Shame.

This wonderful period at Biggin Hill exceeded all my expectations, life was one big party. The 1966 longest day competition was held on the 18th June; I logged 2 hours flying in Chipmunk G-APPK by completing several cross country legs. The idea of this competition was to fly the aircraft as many hours as possible during the official day. Time was deducted for pilot change, refuelling and walk round checks. Time keepers and ground crews were selected from each flying club to provide several teams to cover this long event. Flight and ground safety was paramount for all concerned as moving props can hurt. Biggin Hill never had an accident of any kind during the event. We did lose one aircraft that was forced to land in a field in Surrey due to engine failure. Long walk home and no party. Flairavia won the day.

Chapter Ten

The joint efforts of my wife, Janice, myself in providing coffee for the members meant that I was asked if I would consider becoming the Group's social secretary. I agreed and then increased the variety of snacks. Then we donated the profits from this small venture to Gwyn Russell the then Group Treasurer. This helped to keep the cost of flying our Chipmunk to a minimum. The 600 Squadron Group was operated by the members for the members and this I considered to be a true flying group.

As winter approached the shorter days provided less flying hours which left some of us hanging around waiting at the Flairavia bar to open. November gave us bonfire night and good reason to raid EFG or Alouette, the enemy. We made rocket launchers out of old guttering to attack the opposition, furious battles raged with rockets appearing from all directions. Unfortunately we underestimated the enemy and were beaten off. We had to reform planning new tactics. I was deputised to attack Alouette from the west, what is now Churchill Way, using a launcher for greater accuracy. Just before letting my first rocket go I heard a most amazing loud thud of an explosion coming from EFG area. Turning round I saw a large orange glow coming from the blast pen close by EFG. I fired the first rocket, aiming for the Alouette club house. The rocket was on target until it suddenly veered around the club and headed straight for a fuel bowser parked outside the south east hanger. At full belt the missile hit the bowser and exploded with a great flash. I stopped breathing for a moment, expecting this 5th of November to go down in history. Thank goodness it extinguished shortly after impact. We strapped the guttering to the side of my Mini to make an improvised tank. We hoped this would give us the opportunity to attack several targets on one run. Lighting each rocket with a cigarette gave one the chance to let off up to 3 rockets before the enemy could retaliate. The second run was cut very short by the sight of several missiles coming towards my car, again we had to retreat not wanting my Mini damaged from the impact of the unknown missiles. The team re-assembled in the bar when stories of the night battles would unfold. The red glow I saw was the result of petrol being poured down the air vent of the blast pen followed by a banger. Another raider climbed on the roof of EFG and put two bangers down their chimney. Results: (i)The blast pen was free of spiders and their webs, and (ii) what was left of EFGs chimney wouldn't need cleaning for sometime. The chances of being hit by a rocket was small as you could see them coming and therefore take the necessary evasive action, like run. This childlike behaviour was elaborated on with each story of success.

Biggin Hill Blast Pens

Photo: © Norman Rivett

No, this was not the result of our November rocket attacks but one of the many pens surrounding our airfield. Only a few survived the redevelopment and these now have a preservation order on them. Unfortunately you cannot view this part of our history as the Pens are on the east side and off bounds to all visitors.

Boxing day was a special day in winter when we had the airfield completely to ourselves with no controlling staff and most of the flying clubs taking advantage of a fun day. I did witness some great flying by our pilots, it was a good time to show off aerobatic skills over the airfield. Nine out of ten Boxing days provided fine weather but, as always in the UK, very cold. One pilot so eager to get airborne he decided to take off from his parking position on the South East apron. Consequently he flew past our club, on the taxi way, at good speed. Hot mugs of tea or coffee and turkey sandwiches, made by my wife Janice, were always to hand. We did have central heating in the club shed, it was an ex R.A.F. paraffin burner positioned in the middle of the club running red-hot while making strange disconcerting noises. It used to pulsate reminding me of the sound track from Quatermass , I always said
"One day that bloody thing is going to take us all into the circuit."
One was red-hot on the front and freezing on the rear. So there we were all rotating like a gaggle of penguins. However it was all we had; otherwise we had to wait for more members to arrive, the more bodies we had the warmer it got.

Chapter Ten

As each crew completed a flight the next would step forward to make good use of this beautiful day. This left the other lads to tell of their adventures. Spirits were high with stories of

"There I was upside down with nothing on the clock but the makers name." Jokes galore from Derek Sheffield who had the members in stitches. The day was a great success and then the celebratory wine began to flow. I had already made up my mind not to fly since I wanted to celebrate the holiday in true fashion and make the most of my first glass of wine.

I heard somebody shout.

"Last flight, come on it's still light."

Gwyn looked at me as if to say come on Merchant

"Have you had much to drink Russell?" "None" he replied.

I grabbed my headset from my car and joined Gwyn in the aircraft. I was seated at the back and it was agreed that I should fly the first leg, whatever the first leg was going to be. With run up checks completed I taxied to 23 grass and applied full power. The Chipmunk then took to the cold air like a swan. I followed the circuit patten, climbing to 1500 feet over the airfield heading north. A descending 180° turn put us heading towards our club shed, levelling out I glanced at the airspeed indicator that was reading 130 knots, great, this should wake up all and sundry, then it was over the club with a neat climbing turn.

"Now let me show you how it's done." Said Gwyn.

With that he completed a similar entry but with a steeper descent. I felt a violent bump as we went over the old 600 Squadron hangar, this drew my attention to the airspeed, 160 plus knots, very close to the V&E speed. The Chipmunk's fabric starts to lift if you allow your speed to increase further. We were heading very fast and low for the shed. Gwyn pulled the aircraft into a vertical climb. I felt as if I was taped to the side of a V2 rocket thinking Gwyn would complete his manoeuvre with a stall turn, but no, he pushed the stick hard forward creating a dust bowl in the cockpit and a bump to my head as it met the canopy. This happens when you put the Chipmunk into a negative G, together with fuel starvation followed by silence.

"You moron Gwyn get the nose down, hard." I screamed.

By now we were over the famous Biggin Hill Valley, that would give us the benefit of at least another 300 feet of altitude. Suddenly the engine fired, coming back to life just as I thought mine was about to end. Parking the aircraft we returned to the most enthusiastic welcome from the other members who had witnessed this display.

Chapter Ten

"Did you see that aircraft taxiing by the club as you went over the club for the second run." asked one member.

"No." Replied innocent Gwyn.

I did, even from the back seat, boy, did that chap get a surprise view, or maybe he never saw the oncoming aircraft. Nevertheless I bet he both heard and felt it.

A very pleasant surprise when Diana Barnato Walker walked into 600's introducing herself to me, I knew this lady very well from my cadet days as one of the volunteer Girls Venture Corps pilots and a little of her flying life. This was the first lady that flew with the Air Transport Auxiliary (A.T.A.) from 1941 until 1945 flying both single and twin engine aircraft having over 80 types in her log book recording the delivery 260 Spitfires to the R.A.F. Diana was the first woman to fly faster than sound in the R.A.F. Lightning .T.4 during 1963. She was awarded the MBE in 1965 for service to aviation.

She was a very attractive lady although now in her mid 40's, slim with a stunning smile and black hair. Being attracted to women I did my best to extend her stay in the club, usual thing.

"Would you like tea Maam." I said thinking I was *'Jack the Lad'*.

"That would be most welcome, one sugar please. Been flying all day and please, call me Diana." She replied.

We chatted for sometime about aviation in general and Biggin Hill.

"Very busy Biggin, got to have your wits about you coming in here." She commented.

I chuckled knowing how very strange it must be for visiting aircraft joining the circuit.

To my amazement she suddenly turned her head and said.

"Would you like to come flying with me I have to go to White Waltham, you do not mind flying with my dog, do you?"

I was gob-smacked at such an invitation and realised I'd over cooked the casual laid back bird pulling exercise. Glancing at my watch I said.

"I have an appointment with my Father in less than an hour so on this occasion I'm afraid I shall have to refuse your very kind offer, next time."

Throughout the years I saw Diana on several aviation occasions, the last being 2006, and as in the past she would give me that lovely half smile.

She died 28th April 2008 aged 90 the very day I wrote this page in 2009.

Chapter 11

1967 was a good year flying the Chipmunk G-APPK. Our social life became accepted as the norm, but reflecting on those years it was a unique period of endless enjoyment at a very low cost. 1968 would prove the reality of my flying ability bringing unhappy times. Yet another change would bring more friends, all with a common interest, flying at Biggin Hill.

Joseph J. Merchant 2010

Walking across the south east apron with a few friends one evening, in fact my birthday 7th May 1967. I was dumb struck by the view of a Tiger Moth flying very low, approaching at high speed and completing a beautiful slow roll.

"Did you see that?" Shouted one of the group.

My jaw locked, stuck for words. It was one of County Flying Club's Tigers. Later in the bar we were to find it was Bob Needham's final flight before leaving Biggin for Kenya. As the whole story unfolded we learned that Bob had taken one sixteenth of an inch off the end of one wing and left a 30 foot scrape mark on the concrete taxiway . The ex R.A.F. pilot instructor Eric Hill was in the front seat, probably laughing his head off knowing Eric. The evening turned into one hell of a party, strange when you say "Bye mate", not knowing if we will ever meet again.

Photo: © Barry Wheeler

P-51D Mustang 44-74494 N6356T

This aircraft was originally with 417 Squadron, Royal Canadian Air Force Serial 9237. In 1960 it was sold to the USA and during 1964 it was flown to the UK. In 1967 it was the winner of the King's Cup when owned and flown by Charles Masefield. In 1969 it featured in the film "Patton" and returned to the USA a year later. During the 1980's it carried the name "Iron Ass", today it has the name "Mustang Sally". It is a beautiful example of this thoroughbred pursuit aircraft. This photo from Barry Wheeler also captures the row of flying clubs premises that dominated the south east area during the 1960's, and 70's. The flying clubs are from left to right: 600 Squadron

Flying Group, with   Percival Proctor IV G-ANXR parked outside, wings folded. - Biggin Hill Flying Club - County Flying Club. - Vendair Flying Club. The trees in the background have fond memories for me. During one late evening flight, in G-APPK, I bounced a County Flying Club Tiger south east of Biggin. The normal sounds coming from me would be DUGA - DUGA - DUGA. confirming a kill; not that the Tiger crew would receive my call as they would be on the Gosport communication system rather than radio. My call did confirm to the Biggin tower staff that a kill had been successful, if any of the staff were still on duty that late. Once I was in view of the Tiger he rolled violently to the left, trying to follow would have been futile, and the pilot soon positioned himself on my rear. I had been well and truly out manoeuvred. Peeling away the Tiger headed for the south east area of the airfield descending to almost ground level. I too descended, applied full throttle to follow and was soon catching up. He was heading for the south east apron when suddenly I saw two white puffs of white smoke, burning rubber from his undercarriage as it contacted the apron. I was rapidly closing on the Tiger which was now flying along the taxiway, There was precious little room left for me to avoid a collision, I couldn't turn right or climb as these would be his preferred actions to keep his aircraft within the airfield boundary. I was left with no alternative but to fly to his left, between him and the trees. I had miscalculated the closing speeds of the two machines and had not taken account of the effect of his touch down on his air speed.

Illustration by Nick Seymour 2010

As always we all gathered in the Flairavia bar to talk of the days activities but I didn't meet my opponent. While the passage of time blurred the memory of the event, I realised at the time how lucky I had been. Just two more trees in the row and I might have been sitting among a pile of aluminium and fabric. As to the other pilot, well I always thought it was Mick Ronayne; but on all the subsequent occasions we met I never asked him whether he was the pilot of the Tiger. Then in March 2010 I 'phoned Mick to see if he could remember the incident.

"Very well." He said.

"Who was the other guy in the Chipmunk?" I asked.

"No idea, didn't see the going of him." He said laughing.

"It was me and it's only taken 40 plus years for us to find out." I replied.

Photo: © Norman Rivett

South East Apron 1967

Top left is the Surrey & Kent Club Bar situated in one of the many blast pens that circled the airfield. Note the Lancaster G-ASXX then painted in a night time camouflage with black underside. The Steel House is seen here with a weekend ice cream van positioned on the active entrance to the hangar. The lower left hangar and offices were the offices and class rooms for the Surrey & Kent Flying club. Note the cars parked on the apron

Chapter Eleven

During this period Gwyn Russell suggested he, Janice and I hire a 4 seater and have a small break flying north visiting new airfields that were normally out of the range of clubs activities. Gwyn checked out and hired a Tri-Pacer P22, G-ATXB from our friend Dennis Andrews, it was a heap, but the propeller went round and the wings appeared to be joined to the fuselage. The great day came when we were due to start this long weekend away. First stop was to be Sywell in Northamptonshire. About one hour into flight for some unknown reason, I started to feel very queasy and it soon turned into a panic attack. For the first time in my life I would experience the terrifying fear of flying. I had completely lost all confidence in myself and didn't understand what had come over me. I remember being so frightened, needing to overcome the embarrassment of wanting to get on the ground as soon as possible. I kept asking myself why, what on earth was happening to me to give me this feeling of insecurity. On landing at Sywell I had to leave Gwyn to handle the landing fee, over night parking and making the necessary hotel arrangements for the night.

The following morning the flight to Tollerton proved I had a problem handling this fear. I had heard stories of military pilots being airsick during sorties and learning to live with the problem. Knowing that I didn't want to be in the air was frightening. From Tollerton we flew onto Newton and rested in a hotel for most of the day. I was in no fit state to continue this exercise but had little choice. We returned to Tollerton the next day and during our evening meal, while little was said, we agreed to return to Biggin Hill the following day after the Kings Cup Air Race. I just wanted to get some rest and sleep off this feeling, I felt so bad exhibiting this weakness to my wife and best friend, hoping that by the morning I would return to my old self. Climbing into the Tri-Pacer gave me a terrifying sickly feeling leaving me with no ambitions to fly.

The air race was exciting, my first experience of the Kings Cup I found the last lap a little hair raising as a mixed bunch of aircraft came over the finishing line in what I can only describe as an extremely low unintentional formation of fabric and metal. The weather was deteriorating and soon the visiting aircraft were taxiing their way to the active runway making tracks for home. The weather forecast for the south gave us solid cloud improving in the south. The weather allowed us to climb to 800 feet heading south east to stay well clear of Heathrow. At one point we were flying at 400 being forced down by deteriorating conditions. As the Thames Estuary came into view we turned west to follow the river until Woolwich ferry and then south over Bromley back at Biggin Hill. Back at base nothing was ever said so I never had the opportunity to discuss this strange emotion with another pilot or my wife. I should have talked it through with my good wife Janice, she, I'm sure would have brought my confidence back.

The following week I flew the club's Chipmunk, again; I must be honest, I thought it was never to be the same. I had lost that school boy feeling of elation, now I was frightened and lacking in confidence.

Photo: © David Milstead

Dennis Andrews with Tri-Pacer PA-22 G-ARCC

Photographed on the South-East Camp. West Camp, still in R.A.F. Hands at that time can be seen in the background .

I have seen photographs of this machine dated 2003 when it looked in very good condition. On July 30th 2006 G-ARCC flying from Popham crashed on take off. The Air Accident Investigation summary follows;

"The pilot adopted a very high pitch attitude on take off. The aircraft climbed at a low rate but failed to gain speed. It then stalled, dropped a wing descended into the ground, striking it with a wing tip before somersaulting and coming to rest inverted. All four occupants survived."

Photo: ©·Norman Rivett

Percival P.28 Proctor 1 G-AHNA

Stuart and Janet Hoare with Mum 31ˢᵗ August 1967. Stuart was a highly regarded professional pilot. Janet was one of the most charming, helpful and polite people employed as air traffic controller at Biggin Hill who continued her profession at other airfields for many years. G-AHNA was destroyed 27ᵗʰ December the same year having a force landing in a ploughed field.

My friendship with Barry (Scoop) Wheeler and his wife Susan became addictive spending almost every weekend at the airfield. Talking in the bar Barry agreed with me the airfield needed its own newspaper, a central point of contact for the many clubs and private owners of aircraft we had at Biggin Hill. Aircraft sales, spares, cleaning services, private hire aircraft twins or single, all relied on airfield people knowing which Tom, Dick or Harry provided which service. The stranger had little help other than the bars or hangars to obtain information about Biggin, always providing they knew Tom, Dick or Harry "The Biggin Hill Bugle" was born, unfortunately the cost of production was far too high for a small publication and with limited advertisers the project was shelved until home computers came in reach of most people . J. Bryant took over this project in 2000 for purely social news.

Chapter Eleven

To raise further cash for our small club I negotiated a deal with a local printing company for the sum of £25.00, 5 hours flying, agreeing to apply a large self adhesive sticker to the fuselage of our Chipmunk advertising their services during one of our air shows. The Chipmunk would be parked in the static display in full view of the public plus one airborne circuit at the end of the show. To be confident the sticker would stay in place I applied a 1" adhesive tape to the leading edges, best to safe than sorry. Gwyn Russell agreed to fly in the front, I would sit in the rear my favourite position. I was eager to get this exercise over as the beer would be flowing at the end of the show not wanting to miss the visiting aircrews that on occasions would be taken away to their hotels situated outside Biggin. Their transport time table was very strict, miss your coach and you walk.

With the show over we both made our way to the parked aircraft ensuring the advert was secure, best to safe than sorry. I completed the walk round checks while Gwyn strapped himself in. Taxying to the 21 runway holding point and seeing the many people in the middle if the airfield was a rare sight, both young and old waving to us as Gwyn zigzagged our way to the run up area. Thoughts of my days with 615 rushed through my mind reflecting my excitement as the R.A.F. fighter pilots would acknowledge my salute. Viewing the long line of visiting aircraft waiting instructions from the control tower I counted 14 for line up and take off clearance The tower made a good job clearing the backlog as one aircraft after another took to the air. I was comfortable and felt my confidence was slowly returning. Our take off was uneventful as Gwyn levelled off at 800 feet turning down wind then base leg selecting flaps and speed correction ready for our landing, all was well until a strange sound came to our attention. I could see the self adhesive sheet had started to peel back flapping against the fuselage. Gwyn gave very clear and very loud instructions
"You have control, get the speed back I'm opening the cockpit".
I immediately followed his instructions taking control, well if you could call control meaning the aircraft would respond to your command, it didn't. The control column felt like a vibrating thick jelly and stirring it was the only way to keep control. Not wishing to select the emergency lever for the hood I reduced the speed and maintained a slight nose down attitude. With both of us tugging on the cockpit hood it opened but I didn't know what this action was for when Gwyn released his harness, turned 90° with his knees on his seat thus enabling him to lean out of the cockpit and grab the flapping sticker. There was more of Gwyn on the outside than there was on the inside.

of the aircraft giving me a clear forward view. Control of the aircraft did improve as I turned for finals I felt both unsafe and very sorry that I had arranged this stupid exercise. I landed claiming it was the shortest landing ever made on 21 turning off at the first entry point. Once clear of the runway Gwyn jump out and removed the large sticker ready for the dustbin. Regrets, yes, it was a stupid idea but I wish I could have measured that landing distance.

42 years later I contacted Gwyn to get the flight details as I had failed to enter the flight in my log book, neither had he, however he did comment.

"I was P1 (pilot in command) but you landed as I was otherwise occupied".

I did laugh at that statement. I do remember clearly giving him the privilege of buying the first drink in the bar that night, what a friend, my hero. The results of that sticker peeling off and applying itself to the rudder or elevator could have created more publicity than the original idea.

Photo: © Barry Wheeler

L.A.C. Gwyn Russell R.A.F.

Possibly one of the greatest friends I had in those carefree days at Biggin.

Photo: © Gordon Jones

Inverted - 28th February 1968

Mick Ronayne was lucky to escape injury from this crosswind incident during a training sortie with then student Barry McGrath in G-AOES (T-6056). This aircraft in the hands of 600 Squadron Flying Group beat the 1960 longest day record of 17 hours 47 minutes by Air Touring Flying Club, the originators of this competition, by flying 18 hours 10 minutes in June 1961. Severely damaged again in 1999. ES is now in storage.

Other Tigers from the County Flying Club.

G-ANKB (N-6911) Exported to Canada 1972 as CF-CJW.

G-APFU (EM-879) Based at Goodwood West Sussex.

G-AOBO (N-6473) Under the leadership of Mick Ronayne this aircraft won the 1968 longest day competition, Mick logged over 10 hours flying during this competition, typical of his ability and enthusiasm. The C of A lapsed on 9th October 1969 but 28 years later BO was purchased by John and Shaynne Shaw who lovingly rebuilt it over a period of seven plus years. New C of A issued 10th August 2009 reregistered F-GTBO based in France

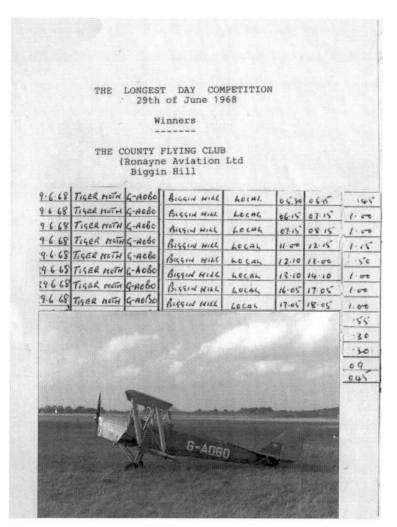

THE LONGEST DAY COMPETITION
29th of June 1968

Winners

THE COUNTY FLYING CLUB
(Ronayne Aviation Ltd
Biggin Hill

9.6.68	Tiger Moth	G-AOBO	Biggin Hill	Local	05.30	06.15	.45
9.6.68	Tiger Moth	G-AOBO	Biggin Hill	Local	06.15	07.15	1.00
9.6.68	Tiger Moth	G-AOBO	Biggin Hill	Local	07.15	08.15	1.00
9.6.68	Tiger Moth	G-AOBO	Biggin Hill	Local	11.00	12.15	1.15
9.6.68	Tiger Moth	G-AOBO	Biggin Hill	Local	12.10	13.00	.50
9.6.68	Tiger Moth	G-AOBO	Biggin Hill	Local	13.10	14.10	1.00
29.6.68	Tiger Moth	G-AOBO	Biggin Hill	Local	16.05	17.05	1.00
9.6.68	Tiger Moth	G-AOBO	Biggin Hill	Local	17.05	18.05	1.00
							.55
							.30
							.30
							09
							045

Winner G-AOBO   Photo: via Mick Ronayne

What must have been one of Mick Ronayne's proudest days 29th June 1968, logging more than 10.30 flying hours during this competition.

Photo: © John Hamlin

Biggin Hill Air Fair May 1968

Photo: © Norman Rivett

F86 Sabre Mk 4 G-ATBF MM19607

It did seem that aircraft arrived at Biggin Hill and ended their lives as scrap. The F86 Mk 4, ex Italian Air Force MM19697, registered G-ATBF was a typical sad story. I remember it, on all three wheels, parked on the South East apron looking well down at heel. It was donated by the Italian Air Force to the Historic Aircraft Preservation Society, Biggin Hill   During 1968 it was transferred to the planned Southend Museum to join the B25 Mitchell "Moviemaker". I was not aware of a Historic Aircraft Preservation Society at Biggin, but they must have had some influence in that they obtained so many ex military machines, why these aircraft were at Biggin and for what reason is unexplained.

Lancaster G-ASXX painted as a night bomber and named "Guy Gibson" the owners added the original serial number NX611 and code HA-P. This aircraft is now at the Lincolnshire Aviation Heritage Centre named "Just Jane" after the comic strip glamour girl from the Daily Mirror newspaper, 1940/50. This aircraft is in beautiful conditions thanks to the people deeply involved in our aviation heritage.

Photo: © Norman Rivett

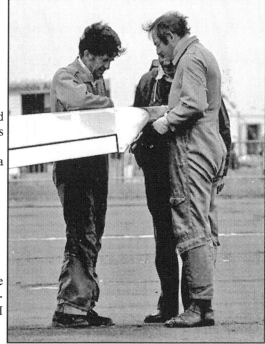

Two   characters and good   friends   Denis Cass and Ian Daziel, "Doc" discussing a technical issue.

Denis Cass had the most enjoyable repeti-tious phrase, and I quote. ------

"D'You know what I mean?"

Photo: Via Rex Nicholls

Chipmunk G-AMXL WD301

Flying instructor Rex Nicholls and assistant instructor Peter Oake shortly after collecting Gordon Jones' "Chippy" from Blackbush, May 1968. Rex enjoyed his Chipmunk flying giving members of E.F.G. who operated Auster's a chance to experience aerobatics. Rex came third in the 1967 Kings Cup Air Race flying S & K Chipmunk G-AOTG. He was a very popular instructor for many years, unfortunately ill health drew a close to his flying career in 2001 when he was the CFI at the Alouette Flying Club. By then he had amassed some 16.500 hours flying from both Croydon and Biggin Hill. Given the opportunity Rex still flies with his many friends but as passenger.

The Chipmunk G-AMXL was lost in March 1978 when it crashed on Dartford Marshes with a fatality. Regardless of the reasons for this accident it is always very sad to lose both crew and aircraft. With the volume of movements at Biggin greater than at Heathrow our safety record was good, although we were a bunch of left over dreamers from WWII chasing imaginary ME109s, blasting our way through the sky with all the bullshit and glamour we could create. Low flying was wonderfully dangerous and great fun. Should you go in a farmer's field clipping corn it was advisable to do this just once, the second time they would get your registration. Low flying, and illegal aerobatics was a £500 fine, for me that was 4 months salary and a shed load of Guinness.

Photo: © Barry Wheeler

1968 Battle of Britain "At Home"

A Meteor back on Biggin Hill. Eleven years since the two Auxiliary Meteor squadrons were disbanded. Photographed left to right are Tony Ansell "The Misguided Muscle", myself, Harry Lindup, ex 600 Squadron ground crew and my then wife Janice. I remember well the chat over this aircraft as Harry dismissed any suggestions that he missed the wages of a weekend airman and the good old days of R.A.F. Biggin Hill.

Weeks before one of the many air shows Janice and I organised a club after air show party, who wants sit in a traffic jam for two hours when you can be entertained with jokes and stories from club members. We purchased the necessary liquids and Janice made snacks of all kinds to ensure members were well fed. Music was a problem and even worse was obtaining speakers until one of our members said he had a couple of spare speakers in his garage assuring us they would be delivered on Saturday morning. He arrived as promised with two of the largest speakers I have ever seen. We unloaded his van storing them in the shed, club house. The weather was low cloud with drizzle that continued throughout the day and by the afternoon not a sparrow had taken to the air. Visitors were giving up and the long queue started to return to their homes empty-handed. The line of traffic passed our club house at snail pace that continued for a couple of hours. You had to feel sorry for the punter having paid good money to see the event only to sit in their cars waiting for the weather to improve. Then came an idea that could cheer us all up and perhaps entertain some of the visitors. Among the pile of long playing records was "Aircraft Sounds". We placed both speakers outside making sure they were protected from the rain and well hidden from our visitors. The first one was the sound of a spitfire flying overhead, volume full on the traffic stopped with people straining their necks to get a glimpse of a flying machine, we did laugh.

"   *"Try the Lancaster."* Shouted one member.

Sure enough over came the sound of the Lancaster. We were all in stitches at the panic on the peoples face trying so hard not to miss the opportunity to see an aircraft. We must have continued this for sometime until the traffic started to thin out and then we managed to get some of the other pilots from County Flying Club, well and truly had by a couple of over sized unwanted speakers.

Turmoil hit 600 Squadron when, at a committee meeting, I objected to one of our members being grounded by our C.F.I. for a non aviation incident. Had the member broken an aviation law, or our aircraft I felt the C.F.I. had a duty to discipline the offending pilots but not for a personal dislike of another pilot. Janice and I worked hard subsidising members flying by running the social side, we needed all the members we could enrol spending money in our club. A registered letter arrived at our private address from the C.F.I. telling me to keep my nose out of the clubs business. I can understand why the C.F.I. didn't like me, we arrived at the club each Saturday morning to clean the club after its use as a hotel during the week. The smell was far from welcoming but by 9.30 we would ceremonially burn all unwanted Y-Fronts while singing 'All you need is love' our favourite song for the C.F.I. Another registered letter arrived informing me that I had been grounded, I found this very hard to take as we both loved the club and its members who reacted in the most unexpected way by staying away or keeping their heads down over this very strange outcome. The following weeks another registered letter from the C.F.I. grounding Janice, he gave no reason leaving us with no option but to move clubs. Joining Flairavia Flying Club flying their Chipmunk G-APPM (WB711). Janice continued her flying scholarship instructed by David Quirk, I continued dipping into my wallet as my days of free flights were well and truly over, no more check outs or jolly flights from the punters, Flairavia was a full time flying school with full time instructors paid by the hours they flew.

Flairavia Flying Club became the social centre on Biggin Hill attracting many characters from all walks of live from tramps to doctors. The only thing that was infectious was the laughter.

True Characters from Flairavia Flying Club

Photo: © via Mike Hardy

Doug Gilbert (T.F.G.) Roy Sanders (P.1.G) Mike Hardy (Messer)

Chapter Eleven

Chapter 12

Having lost the spirit of 600 Squadron Flying Group along with some of its members, 1969 was the year of change both for my ever increasing passion for Biggin Hill and of my dislike for my employer, W. F. Stanley of New Eltham was now managed by morons. My efforts coupled with those of many colleagues could not save this great British institution from self destruction . Time to give up and move on.

Joseph J. Merchant 2010

Less than a year after Janice and I had left the 600 Squadron Flying Group
it was announced that financial problems had forced it to close. The very
thing we stood for and helped financially had finally put an end to this great
flying group. I truly believe there had also been someone behind the scene
planning to end this last R.A.F. flying connection. There were, after all, a
number of non ex R.A.F. personal in the group, of course, I could be wrong.

Photo: © Pilots Pals

The last days of 600 Squadron Flying Group 1969

Although my wife and I had made new friends in Flairavia Flying Club it
was heart breaking to witness what had once been a Group heaving with
flying and social activity, now reduced to a scene of dereliction. The club
locked up, G-APPK out of C of A looking very sad and even the grass was
dying.

Thanks to the efforts of Flairavia principal, David Porter, the club's activities made for good public relations being recorded in the British press. A
Cooper Racing car driven by Trevor Shatwell was sponsored by the club.
David's enthusiasm saved the day of the locomotive 'Black 5' No.45110
from the scrap merchants christening it 'R.A.F. Biggin Hill'. Today this fine
example of the steam era can be seen at the The Severn Valley Railway.
David organised a party of people to locate Sqn. Ldr. Tom Gleave's Hurricane

P3115 shot down on 31st August 1940 when returning to base at R.A.F. Kenley after a massive enemy air attack on Biggin Hill. The remains of P3115 Hurricane were found on Mace Farm in Cudham just outside Biggin Hill. I remember sipping ale in the Flairavia bar when the party returned with a very muddy Merlin engine and parked it against the wall of the club. Again it was down to David to get the press to provide a substantial frame and stand for this prize that is now on permanent display at the Imperial War Museum Duxford. Sqn. Ldr. Tom Gleave sustained severe burns prior to bailing out of his stricken Hurricane and underwent plastic surgery by the famous pioneering surgeon Archie McIndoe. In July 1941, at the Queen Victoria Hospital, the Guinea Pig Club was formed with Archie McIndoe as president and Tom Gleave as vice-president and founder member. Hence the naming of Flairavia's first Beagle Pup's G-AVZO "Guinea Pig". Flairavia went onto win the longest day competition on the 21st June 1969 in this aircraft flying 17 hours 30 minutes and 15 seconds out of a possible 17 hours 36 minutes.

30th July 1969

Another great publicity stunt by Flairavia was the flight training and solo flight in one day by Penny Brahms the film and TV actress in Beagle Pup G-AWDX.

Instructor David Quirk gave 7.45 hours flight training to achieve this one day solo exercise. Good news for the club and for Biggin Hill Airport as this achievement made the national press.

Photo: © Norman Rivett

The ultimate Instructor and Gentleman

During our time with Flairavia Flying Club we met more members and new instructors; Paul Shires was one of my favourite types full of fun and sharing in the day-today training with David Quirk. The big day for my wife was having successfully completing her G.F.T. (General Flight Test). I was so very proud of Janice completing the Private Pilots Licence course bearing in mind both her petite size and having chosen to fly an ex R.A.F basic trainer. The club recognised her determination by rewarding her with the Woman's Award for the year; presented to her by Michael Aspel the well known TV presenter at the annual Flairavia dinner.

I joined Alouette Flying Club flying their Chipmunk G-AOZV (WD290) possibly one of the finest club Chipmunks I had the pleasure to fly, it was a very tidy aircraft. The social life at Alouette was a little dangerous with the odd strip show and some very good parties. I enjoyed the club and its members and at one time I was invited to join the committee but having experience with 600 Squadron Flying Group I declined their offer

.The C.F.I. Of Alouette was Don Peach one of the finest gentlemen I had the pleasure of knowing. One of their assistant instructors was Frank Lawson yet another gentleman who loved his flying and his fun time.

Photo: © Pilots Pals

G-AOZV with my new Austin 1300 GT

I took this image from the old control tower on the South East Apron when you could drive almost anywhere on the airport particularly if the airport staff had retired for the day making their way to one of the many bars.

The airport, airfield, call it what you like was just one big wonderful place where people from all walks of life would come together and fly or to talk about flying. We never thought or discussed authority, it never came up that we could lose this paradise one day and as far as all concerned this was our historical and sacred playground and nobody was to disturb our leisure.

10th August 1969 proved an interesting day for Robin Philips, one of Biggin Hill's part time controllers, and private owners. Flying as passenger in the National Air Guard's Aer Macchi AL60 G-AXEZ over Yarmouth viewing a water sport event the aircrafts engine spluttered and stopped. Having no choice but to ditch in this vast area of water, the crew and passengers got extremely wet. The many vessels viewing this event set sail to rescue our aviators from the certain jaws of death. All were collected safely with Robin being pulled aboard a boat that soon after setting sail for the shore collided with another vessel making both un seaworthy, he was immediately trans-ferred to yet another boat. By the time the boat docked to unload this very wet aviator the police were waiting to transfer him to the local hospital for a routine check over. During the unnecessarily high speed dash to the hospital the police car was involved in a collision with another vehicle making it a hat trick day for Robin, as a passenger in all three accidents in a single day was evaluating the chances of being place in the hands of another complete moron that under no circumstances should be in command of any metal or fabric that has any form of power. Clearly Robin was pleased to have survived the day but had second thoughts catching the train for his return journey to London.

Art Legg

All our air shows at Biggin Hill were great fun be it Jock Maitland's Air Fair or the Royal Air Force "At Home" Battle of Britain day in mid September. 19th Sep-tember 1969 Battle of Britain day. Unbe-known to me a certain Flight Lieutenant Art Legg flew Vulcan BII XM656 for R.A.F. Biggin Hill "At Home"Ten years would elapse before I had the pleasure of meeting Art who, at that time, was posted to M.o.D. London with accommodation at R.A.F. Biggin Hill.

Chapter Twelve

For me things always happen in September, not my favourite month as the nights draw in and the temperature can drop to a premature chill reminding us of what is to come however a visit to Ashdown Forest was great witnessing mother nature preparing herself for yet another new beginning.

My life with W. F. Stanley was coming to an end as my patience was completely exhausted trying to deal with the day-today errors of the so called management who were nothing but a bunch of idiots performing their mundane paper work duties of production statistics. Production was up and that was to the benefit of the paper mills. We had so many charts it reminded me of a scene from Churchill's War Cabinet office.

I came across a very small advertisement in the local paper for the position of assistant buyer for a printers supplier in Orpington. I applied by letter and within a couple of days received a reply requesting I attend an interview. It was rather strange as on arrival I was informed that this was in fact the second round of interviews for the position. I began to think I had more chance of flying inverted through Blackwall Tunnel than gaining this position. Being the last to be seen of six other gentlemen I was eventually called into the interviewing office to meet the buyer, Mr Tony Gregory and accountant, Mr Bill Christie, both very pleasant people. I realised it was more of a chat than an interview. Mr Christie explained that the company had dealings in Chemicals, imported printing machinery and sundries. What did I know about chemicals, not very much. I thought White Spirit was a ghost from the Hammer Film Studios. Now something the company did have and attracted my attention was a computer, I had read a little about these advanced accounting toys that could be a winning asset to any company's purchase office. I was very nervous knowing I was far from qualified for such a position but I had to get out of the whirlpool of misery I had endured for so long. Showing my appreciation for their time I said my farewell, leaving the building very happy, there was an air of difference here, yes I like this very much. A few days passed and I received the good news I had been successful in my application and would I telephone to confirm my starting date. This was to be a new start for me away from that bunch of morons that couldn't organise a piss-up in a brewery. My starting date coincided with the move to our new home in Bursdon Close, Sidcup, a two up, two down end of terrace for which we had to pay a deposit of nearly a one thousand pounds. Having a place to rest your head after a days work is a must but it did break us financially for a few months.

Leaving W. F. Stanley was in a way sad but so necessary for my health and sanity. My new employment, Algraphy Ltd, Murray Road. My new home in Sidcup was closer to the company and closer to Biggin Hill. The very first day with this new company I was to witness a very different type of men and women working in unison as a team. Peter Brown was the warehouse manager, to see him organise the unloading of goods in was remarkable. This Sergeant Major type had the total respect of his team, goods were checked in and cleared in minutes, the loading bays always ready for the next delivery. You could smell the success of this business, the happiness of all the employees was so obvious. I shall never forget the elegant elderly chairman, Mr Potter, who's interest in the employees was genuine and sincere. My boss, Tony Gregory, was a encyclopaedia on legs he was so intelligent but hated his job and at 5 o'clock he was off regardless of the outstanding work, not a lazy man but certainly not happy in purchasing. Three months after joining this wonderful company I was offered the top job with Tony being transferred to the export office. I turned this opportunity down several times until I could get assurance from my top boss I could do it my way with no interference from other offices. He agreed and work started it earnest applying basic purchasing documentation of authority that few of the employees objected to. I would win the day and success came with long hours and excellent hard working staff .

Happy working conditions.

I made a note in my photo album: *"Their loyalty was unique, the work was hard, the fun was unbelievable. The company benefited financially"*.

One of the first things I was forced to do was employ a new printing company as the existing supplier failed to deliver on time or even care. I had chemical production lines held up for simple things like labels. Little did I know that after telling the supplier they were no longer required I was to learn our sales manager had a interest with them. I interviewed three printers selecting the middle priced company, Petts Wood Printing Ltd. in St Mary Cray. We organised our printing such that deliveries were made in 5 to 6 hours. The day-today requisitions needed attention speeding up their progress, reducing costs. The next big problem was the annual stocktaking that demanded hours of price searching and the mathematical problem when it came to pricing all the aluminium sheets, our raw material for litho plate production. My ex boss,Tony, completed this endless task with a slide rule surely this was a job for an electronic calculator. Permission granted by the boss I purchased a model what resembled a small piano at the cost of over £500.00. The faster our office came up with solving problems the more work we were given. Treat your staff with respect and see what you receive in return.

Back to Biggin Hill with a few bob in my pocket.

Photo: © Norman Rivett

Known as the "Cloth Bomber"

G-APPL Percival Prentice attempted the London to Sydney air race but was force to retire in Southern France. PL was collected by Coby and flown back to Biggin Hill. January 1970.

Chapter 13

Life should be easy and I guess it was for me, new home, new job and not being afraid of hard work all seemed to fall into place. Flying Chipmunk G-AOZV was a joy knowing my confidence was returning slowly. I was proud again but every turning year gave me both good and bad news.

Joseph J. Merchant 2010

The success of Algraphy, my new employer, was very obvious, you could almost smell the sweet odour of wealth. Both the litho plate and chemical production lines had few failures or rejection hence the continued high margins of profits all thanks to the entire team of the employees. One man who will always have a special place in my memory was John Jackson, manager and chemist of the chemical manufacturing division at Margate, what a wonderful human being. Rumours circulating the company of a take-over were non stop. One bid, that all and sundry seem to know, had been rejected at just under one million. The biggest competitor manufacturing similar products was a company trading as Howson Ltd.. They were based in Leeds and a subsidiary of the Crabtree Group, in turn part of Vickers. Eventually Vickers made an offer that was accepted by the Algraphy board. Shame Vickers didn't approach me I could have reduced their outlay by some considerable amount. Initially the acquisition had little affect on the day-today running of both Algraphy and Howson. One big advantage of being involved with the Vickers organisation was their H.Q. facility at Millbank in London. Their extensive data of world affairs was useful to those who took the trouble to enquire.

Vickers were so impressed with their new acquisition that the chairman, Sir Peter Matthews, arranged to visit our premises. The usual orders from management " Make sure your office looks tidy and busy", busy, we didn't have time for a public relation exercise, we had plants relying on our word of a delivery time and date to meet their demands. The big day came for the chairman's visit. It must have been such a boring routine for him shaking hands with so many people and asking if all was well. My reply was

"All is very well Sir, thank you, but I do have an interest in your Spitfire parked under overgrown foliage covered in birds droppings at South Marston, shame such a beautiful aircraft is left in that state. "
His reply was instant.
"Leave that to me, thank you. " Shaking my hand goodbye.
The expression on my bosses face was not a happy one.

January 1970 work started on the restoration of LA226 at South Marston and on completion it was then parked outside the works . During one of my visits to the head office at Millbank in 1977 LA226 was parked at the entrance to the building. During 1984 LA226 was transferred to the Biggin Hill Memorial Chapel as a gate guardian. Since 1987, the aircraft has been in an R.A.F. Storage facility and is now being restored at R.A.F. Cosford

Photo: © Wojciech Luczak

Spitfire Mk21 LA226 at Millbank, London.

The Algraphy public relations manager, Gerald Tutton, wanted a story for the Vickers News. He asked me and the production director Peter Davidson, who also held a private pilots licence, to fly in formation for an air to air photo shoot , Good idea for the Vickers News maybe, but flying in formation with the unknown quantity of a 60 hour pilot flying a Rallye, led me to insist that I would formate on him in the Chipmunk G-AOZV. The flight was great fun, it made a very good editorial for the company's paper and encouraged others to take up the sport. Later I would have the pleasure of meeting the Vickers News editor, Richard Thomas.

I continued flying G-AOZV enjoying every trip, not much dog fighting going on as the County Flying Club had reduced its fleet size and many of the other clubs were now flying a more modern aircraft. This produced what we called "Arm Chair Pilots". Get behind one of these chaps in the circuit and you would find yourself over Bromley turning base leg.

The Alouette's social life was great fun and well known for the strip shows that attracted a few people from other clubs. The brick built club house situated just off the south east apron, was far to small to accommodate the number of guests who crammed in and were forced to use every square inch of the clubs benches, floor, or standing on the back board of the benches.

I always hung from one of the steel supporting beams protruding from the ceiling with my feet secured on the back of a bench. .The noise produced by the gentlemen was amazing with screams of.

"Get em on."

Boos and cheers as the ladies did their best trying to deal with the din and within such a small area. Off would come the bra only to increase the deafening screams of excitement as the young lady would continue to remove more of her lower garments . I could never understand the point of music, it was impossible to hear a thing other than the audience. Then came the break for refreshing our pint glass, that took at least 30 minutes then back to floor show. On my return, pint in hand, the woman minder who was roughly 4ft 3in short asked me

"Enjoying the show boy." If ever I said the wrong thing this was it, my reply being far from sincere.

"I'm feeling a little glow in my lower region and hoping it increases."

With that she grabbed my sausage and two veg and squeezed. I immediately had a may day situation with my beer, I did yell.

"No" trying to get my priorities right, beer, lower regions, pain, oh the pain. She let go saying.

"You won't get much heat out of that tonight."

The surrounding members were laughing their heads off suggesting that if I wanted to perform I'd best do it in the middle of the club for all to witness. Back on my perch hanging from the ceiling out of reach of the little devil the second half was more exciting as the ladies actions encouraged the lads to create mayhem, the noise grew to such a pitch with the lads cheering and stamping their feet, banging on the wall. The long bench supporting half the club opposite me collapsed under the weight of so many who were in turn supported by the curtains and rails, all ended covered by dusty curtains drenched in beer. The remaining members roared with laughter as this bundle of bodies were trying to sort themselves out. It took sometime for the dust to settle bringing the show to a stand still until the lads could reorganise themselves removing all the debris and recharging their glasses. More screams of delight as the girls removed their wrappings

"Get em off, no, put em on."

The evening was brought to a premature end as one of the members put his cigarette out, guess where, when one of the young ladies stuck her undercarriage in his face. Bad news that. Barry Wheeler and I must have been the last sipping our ale and the last to leave what looked like a battle scene from a war movie.

Back at work I received a telephone call from the editor of Vickers News , Richard Thomas, requesting a meeting at Biggin Hill for possible further photographs and editorial on my hobby. Arrangements made.

Photo: © Vickers News

Richard Thomas and myself with G-AOZV.

Both Richard and his charming wife spent most of the day at Biggin Hill enjoying the flying and the social life that I had. Richard was in awe of my life style asking me endless questions on general aviation, that, thankfully I could answer. I found that most people who have never been involved with flying were under the impression it was a mystical world far beyond their reach. After 50 minutes flying over Kent performing some basic aerobatic manoeuvres I then let Richard take control ,this pleased him no end. My instruction went well, he banked both left and right closed the throttle and descended applied the power and climbed then I asked him some simple aviation questions like

"What is the white fluffy thing in the sky?."
"A cloud." He replied with a giggle
"You sure your not a pilot you seem to know a lot about aviation".
"Have you ever been serious Joe?" He asked.
"No,gives me headaches." I replied.

To complete their day I gave Richard's wife a short flight to allow them to compare notes on the journey home and of course make ready the editorial for the company's newspaper. As always after flying there is the ritual of liquid consumption, not that I was thirsty but the thought of a few pints of Guinness did please me. All on company expenses of course, well I was flying a company executive and his wife. Just another great day at Biggin.

Photo: © Vickers News

Happy Days G-AOZV

This is the best photograph of ZV ever taken thanks to Richard Thomas having parked himself on the end of runway 11 to get this ground to air shot.

14th June 1970 Alouette Flying Club arranged for their club members to have an away day at Shoreham in Sussex. The idea being to position the aircraft away from Biggin Hill with members meeting up to fly from a different airfield allowing them to cover the south west coast that included the Isle of Wight at reduced cost. Every slot was take up very quickly with a committee member requesting that I fly ZV back to Biggin at the end of the day. I loved late evening flying and if you were a little late arriving at Biggin it made no difference other than you could perform a few aerobatics over the field before landing. I was never in trouble for such antics and considered this a salute to my heroes, the same airfield, the same sky but a very different time.

Photo: © Ken Elliott

1970 Air Fair
Two Royal Navy Sea Vixens XJ572 and taking on fuel XJ576

For me this formation was the highlight of the show, never had I seen such low level exercise being performed with such close precision.

Photo: © Richard Dayman

Cessna 150K Aerobat N8308M Demonstrator 1970
One step up for the armchair pilots of Biggin, pretty machine.

Chapter Thirteen

The 2rd of August 1970 was a special day with a few events that would engrave themselves in my memory. I was to fly ZV for the last time, flying along the south coast occasionally seeing one of my fellow aviators on track for an unknown destination hopefully enjoying the many beautiful views of Kent and Sussex coast. Landing back at Biggin I taxied to the refuelling bowser making ZV ready for the next member.

The weather was fine, I remember leaning on the wall of the control tower viewing the active runway 11 watching a Aero Commander take off, as it came almost parallel with me I saw the right hand undercarriage wheel over take him, bouncing down the runway. *"EPIC"* I screamed attracting everyone's attention away from the potentially dangerous situation of a wheel travelling at high speed disappearing beyond the airfield boundary. Obviously the pilot would have no idea he had left part of his flying machine on the ground, but would have been informed by the tower who must have had a grand stand view of this unfolding epic. The aircraft started to circle the airfield above circuit height, then the aviation chatter started

"Well if I was him I would take it down to Manston" said one chap.

R.A.F. Manston in those days was the emergency landing aerodrome that had a facility for such an emergency by mean of laying a carpet of foam on the runway .

"Bloody expensive exercise that." replied his mate.

All sorts of ideas of how to get this aircraft down without too much damage were being discussed by the group that by now had swollen in numbers, A shout from the tower

"We're' putting him on 03"

.Photo via Chris de Vere Jr.

The scene was one from the Battle of Britain with Pilots running to their cars to get a look at what could be an epic.

I arrived at the end of 03 and parked my car to the left of the centre line of the runway along with all the other on lookers.

"Who's flying it?" I heard one of the group ask.

"It's Chris de Vere with friends" came a reply.

No problem there I thought since Chris had many hours flying experience on many types. As Chris flew overhead we all started to run down the runway and saw the Aero Commander kiss the concrete of 03. I soon came across the initial point of contact and picked up pieces of red plastic from the cover of the anti collision warning light from the underside of the fuselage. By this time the aircraft had come to rest, all was well. In the bar that night I placed the unwanted pieces of the red light cover into an ashtray.

Photos: via Chris de Vere Jr.

Aero Commander G-ASJU

Chris de Vere inspecting the right undercarriage leg after making a successful belly landing on 03.

The aircraft was ready to fly the following day as little damage was caused by this incident.

Chapter Thirteen

As very few accidents happened at Biggin Hill every small incident was great entertainment for all the club members. Another epic was created by a student on his solo flight who was experiencing a few problem landing his aircraft, his circuits becoming more of a cross county flight than a single solo exercise of one circuit. Time went by as more pilots gathered to witness this unfortunate student that seemed to have a great fear in meeting planet Earth, evidence shown by his increasing time to complete a single circuit, other aircraft would be forced to follow him almost reaching Bromley to turn into base leg, many pilots got tired of his performance and simply turned in letting him go on his merry way. Again he was on his final approach all looking well for a text book landing. No, he hit the ground like a ton of you know what immediately applying full power for yet another 8 minutes circuit. Inside that cockpit was possibly a very frightened young man who was going through hell, little did he know he was entertaining a large group of people commenting on his performance.

"He will come down eventually, he's going to run out of fuel." said one chap.

"No, call in the ack-ack boys and shoot the bugger down it's more entertaining." Replied another to the laughter of the group.

The student eventually landed parking his aircraft clear of the runway, and stayed there for sometime.

"Bars open, anyone buying." Cried out one of the group.

The gathering dispersed very quickly. On reflection I don't remember the bars on Biggin Hill having strict licensing hours, clubs were open or closed, winter playing its part in our social drinking due to the lack of pilots in the short winter days of club and private flying.

As I have said September is, for me, a bad month, the turning of the season and bad news to follow. On the 11th 1970 the highly experienced test pilot "Pee Wee" Judge lost his life in the WA-117 Gyroplane G-AXAR at Farnborough, Initial reports stated this accident was caused by pilot error , in fact it was due to negative "GS". "Pee Wee" was a fast jet pilot and at the time I found it strange he was flying this exaggerated plastic kit, very different from his days with 615 at Biggin Hill. He was a good man.

Another piece of sad news was the closure of the County Flying Club during September 1970. The following is Mick Ronayne's view of his very special flying club that provided flying training and endless enjoyment for all the members and friends.

The County Flying Club (Ronayne Aviation Ltd.)
By
Mick Ronayne

The County Flying Club was formed after the closure of Croydon Airport in 1959. Their was, at that time a general exodus of aviation companies, flying clubs and private owners from Croydon to Biggin Hill.

The County Flying Club started life in the early 60's as the Progressive Flying Club having only one aircraft - Tiger Moth G-AOES. This wonderful old aeroplane was to stay with me throughout the life of Ronayne Aviation, she was built in 1943 by the Morris Motors Company at Cowley. The next priority was accommodation; this was provided by the airport manager Roy Taylor "Pipe" and consisted of a caravan behind the hangar on the south east apron. We eventually moved onto a wartime dispersal bay, erected a prefab of wartime vintage that was soon knocked into offices, a briefing room and most important of all a bar.

The club owned five aircraft; four Tiger Moths and one Miles Gemini. We also operated other aircraft that were owned by other clubs who were affiliated to us. For example the Metropolitan Police Flying Club operated a Condor, the Civil Service Flying Club a Bolkow Junior and the University of London Flying Club an Auster. County F.C. provided the instructional staff with myself as C.F.I. The Civil Service F.C. eventually had their own instructors when the famous or infamous Knight brothers appeared on the scene.

The dispersal bay can be seen in this image, circa 1964. The Percival Proctor G-AOAR was owned by Roger Barham. The club house and work shop, at the rear, housed an Auster V undergoing restoration. Flying ops consisted mainly of training for the private pilots licence (PPL) and associated ratings such as night flying and aerobatics

Photo: © Ian MacDonald

Looking back on my first visit to Biggin Hill in 1960 little did I know of the great impact it would have on my life. Biggin Hill seemed a strange place at first; the entrance, for instance, being a five barred gate permanently in the open position. It was not until I had visited the Surrey & Kent bar that I became aware of the incredible mixture of characters with whom I was destined to share a major part of my life. Biggin Hill in the 1960's and 1970's was unique place: with its mixture of ancient and modern aeroplanes. serving the same sort of flying clubs. People went around in ex R.A.F. Sidcote, and other, flying suits and goggles; on the other hand we had the best suit and nav-bag brigade. I was fascinated to see how friendships were made between, for example bank managers and chaps who worked at factory bench level. There was also a fantastic social scene with endless parties such as 'Vicars and Tarts' and the like. The highlight of these nights was often a performance by Roy Sanders, (P.1.G), a born comedian who did miming to; Shirley Bassey's "Big Spender" and Victor Borge.

Photo: © Pilots Pals

Roy Sanders "P.1.G"

The fun was endless, Roy being a great source of continuous entertainment Shown above is Roy on one of Shirley Bassey's high notes.

To wind up my description of life on Biggin Hill Airport would not be complete without mentioning the car races round the aerodrome perimeter track. These were usually held in the early hours of the morning after being turned out of the one of the bars after a party, all participants being 'Brahms and liszt'. The starting and finishing point was a white line opposite the control tower on the South East apron. All sorts of vehicles entered from Charles Daniel's Ferrari to Mini's. It was extremely dangerous and there were, unfortunately, a few accidents. Even the police came on the airfield to watch; they must have loved blood sport. As a flying instructor I often sat in the cockpit of a Tiger Moth first thing in the morning with a bit of a hangover (nothing dangerous mark you). What was my first detail, you've guessed it, spinning. It was not all like that, a lot of damned hard work went into training and quite a number of my pupils went onto become R.A.F. Pilots, airline and other commercial pilots. There are still a few about to this day, some retired. This, was of course, was what it was all about; work hard and play hard. I'm afraid it will never be the same again at Biggin Hill.

Mick Ronayne 2010

Photo: © Via Mick Ronayne

Mick with Bolkow Junior G-ASFS

Photo: © Via Mick Ronayne

Tiger Moth G-AOES

In closing, the final days of the County Flying club would not be complete without including a few images of the antics the members were treated to, all in the name of enjoyment. Above Mick Ronayne at the controls with Jim Newman paying his respects to the control tower flying down runway 29.

Photo: © Pilots Pals

One of the many 'Vicars & Tarts' parties held at Biggin. Doug Gilbert admiring the outfit of the beautiful Beverly, just one of the fun loving women that attended these frequent celebrations. Trying to find a photo of Doug without a filled glass was almost impossible, he was another great source of entertainment with stories from his charmed life. He did consider work a four letter word and never to be used in female company.

Photo: © Vickers News

G-AOZV (WD290) on finals for 29

Note the old Algraphy company logo of the engine cowling. This photo shoot was used in yet another article for the Vickers News.

Exhausted

After one hour of aerobatic training I did suffer tiredness wondering how the R.A.F. lads handled these exhausting exercises up to three times a day during the air show display season.

Photo:© Pilots Pals

This beautiful aircraft was one of the many Chipmunks at the"Air Service Training Ltd" later reformed as "The College of Air Training, Hamble." ZV was one Chipmunk that operated from 1957 until 1967. During 1971/2 it was sold and exported to the U.S.A. as N83778.

Chapter Thirteen

Chapter 14

My employment and the responsibilities that went with it absorbed much of my time. The addition to our family, gave me even more responsibility but brought priceless happiness. The changing range of training aircraft at Biggin meant that I became an irregular social visitor rather than a regular aviator. Tiger Moths and Chipmunks were being replaced by the more modern trainers, not my cup of tea. The Alouette Flying Club obtained the Victa Airtourer an exciting prospect.

Joseph J. Merchant 2010

I was now fully committed to my career though the responsibility was a great challenge to my as yet underdeveloped management skills. However my continuous hard work and determination coupled with the loyalty of my staff bore fruit. The purchasing office became both effective and efficient; sometimes to the envy of other offices and occasionally evoking unnecessary feelings. However, all departments require the services of the purchasing office at sometime and I insisted that purchase requisitions be processed strictly in accordance with the methods I had introduced. If my office was to be able to satisfy the requirements of others then they would have to adhere to requisition policy and apply through correct channels together with appropriate financial authority. I had to balance the needs of the individual and the well being of the Company. My strict policy of no back-handers from suppliers was the only mistake I made in all my years with Vickers. I could have been financially comfortable for many years.

On the 2rd May 1971 I was to check out on Airtourer G-AWRT the replacement for Alouette's Chipmunk G-AOZV, the aircraft I had flown some nine months previously. After a 45 minute flight I successfully checked out with assistant instructor F. Lawson though not before almost frightening him to death on finals. The aircraft in front crashed on 23, the tower promptly instructed all aircraft to land on 21. A fist full of throttle followed by a sharp S turn put us number one for the mile long main runway, he wasn't impressed saying.
"You should have gone round, don't ever do that again."
However we had the air speed for such a low level manoeuvre and I found myself apologising for the speedy action that I had found very exciting

Photo: © John Wilkinson

Alouette Flying Club at the Biggin Hill Air Fair 1971

Photo: © Barry J. Collman

Rothmans Aerobatic Team 1971

The envy of our many pilots at Biggin Hill was this first civilian full time aerobatic team that would continue to entertain our visitors for a decade. The founder and leader of this team was the 1971 British National Aerobatic Champion winner "Manx" Kelly his team initially flying the Stampe SV-4.

It was during the 1971 Air Fair that I met Douglas Gilbert in the Surrey and Kent Club twiddling his thumbs as if he was in deep thought scheming up one of his doggy deals. He had recently been upset by one of his local councillors and determined that he would put the councillor's house up for sale, he placed an advert in his local paper reading;

"3 bedroom detached house in a secluded area close to local shops. Phone. between 1am and 5am due to working hours. Ethnic minorities welcome. Quick sale £34.000." The price was well under market value and gave Doug the satisfaction his councillor would receive calls in the middle of night from all and sundry. Moral, never upset Gilbert; as he never allowed himself to be beaten. On another occasion he was very angry with somebody who had a prize lawn, Doug purchased some 4" nails, painted them green and at night placed them at irregular intervals in the lawn. The tales of Doug would make a great film.

"Hi Doug, what's in your dreams today?" I asked.

"My dear boy, thoughts of paradise stream through my mind I yearn to travel the world again." He replied reaching for his large whisky.

During his R.A.F. career as a fighter pilot flying Spitfires he served in the UK, Malta and in 1945 travelled to Australia via the U.S.A. ready for the final push on Japan, The Japanese surrendered before Doug saw any action in the Pacific. He returned to the UK and was demobed in 1946. . During our brief chat at the bar in walked a police motor cyclist asking for the whereabouts of a Mr. Douglas Gilbert. Doug immediately responded saying
" He's returned to Australia. "
"Thank you. " replied the officer making a record in his notebook. Then the unbelievable happened when Doug started talking to the police officer about his motor bike days stating he had ridden many different types but never had the pleasure of riding the police model. Douglas ordered yet another large whisky and invited the police officer to join him with a cup of tea that was accepted with much appreciation by now his new friend. It took only a few minutes for Doug to be putting both the policeman's glove and helmet and then to be seen riding the police motor bike up and down the south east apron waving to his many friends. That was Douglas Gilbert (TFG) for you.

Yet another great character I had the pleasure of meeting was Alan Humphreys, a master of car and motor cycle restoration. At one time he had the most amazing collection of Triumph bikes. I have seen rust buckets that would be discarded by most but once in Alan's hands it was like watching a Walt Disney production in slow motion, the end result being a beautiful vehicle restored to such a high standard. All the years I knew Alan he was the most helpful person who loved his fun times but like myself a great critic of the morons than were running our country into the ground.

Leopard in his Tank

One of Alan's pets was his Leopard called Ghia seen here before a flight from Biggin Hill. Ghia, renamed Growley, was taken over by Miss Stella Fenton a Director of the Nottingham Sherwood Zoo.

Photo: © Via Alan Humphreys

Alouette Flying Club had a lease agreement with Glos Air, the distributors for the New Zealand Victa Airtourer. During 1971 I flew 5 different aircraft, G-AWRT - G-ATCK - G-AXIX - G-AXAJ - G-AZHI and yet the club only operated one aircraft at a time. Glos Air obviously looking after its southern customer bearing in mind Alouette's agreement contained minimum hours per month so the turn round of aircraft was in the interest of both parties.

Photo: © Via Don Peach

12th December 1971

Alouette's Chief Flying Instructor Don Perch congratulates student pilot Malcolm Doling on completing his first solo in G-AZHI. Don continued as C.F.I. for may years, a gentleman who was dedicated to flight training. Malcolm completed his P.P.L and became a committee member. The club had an alcohol licence but never a full time publican, trust was a must in those days for all members.

More responsibility arrived on the 2nd February 1972 when my wife gave birth to our first son, Gary, at the Queen Mary's Hospital in Sidcup. This addition would bring me endless happiness the making of our family, not forgetting the family dog, a cross Black Labrador Alsatian appropriately named Brandy. Coincidentally the 2rd February 1917 is the official opening date for Biggin Hill as an R.F.C. airfield.

One further Airtourer that Alouette had during my time with them was G-AYMF, this I flew on a check flight with Mick Ronayne on the 24th April 1972. I didn't log any further flights after May 1972, having lost interest in the whole scene due to my commitment to my family and career. Had the Chipmunk still been around I feel sure I would have continued flying for many years as my financial situation was healthy.

The Alouette Victa Glos-Air Airtourer aircraft 1971/72.

G-AWRT 115/T2   Damaged beyond repair 23rd Nov. 1973.
G-ATCK 100   Crashed Biggin Hill 25th August 1974.
G-AXIX 150/T4   Flying at Shobdon as "The Lean Machine".
G-AXAJ 150/T4   Flying at Staverton.
G-AZHI 150/T5   Flying at Rochester.
G-AYMF T6/24   Crashed Lands End 9th July 1972.

Photo: © Pilots Pals

Victa Glos Air Airtourer G-AZHI

This is the only photo I have of my days with the Alouette Flying Club. Gone had the flying suit, leather head-set and flying gloves, gone had that distinctive odour from the Gypsy Major engine that powered both the Chipmunk and Tiger Moth. The Australian designed Airtourer was a good aircraft made by the lawn mower company, Victa, in New Zealand and later in Australia. The story of this aircraft is worth a read bringing light on the U.S.A.'s way of business and the lack of interest from the Australian Government.

The Bolkow BO209 Monsun was introduced by Air Touring during the early 70's. The 'Flight' test gave this machine a very good report ending *"The Monsun certainly offers something distinctively different, apparently without a great cost penalty"*. G-AYPE is still based at Biggin Hill.

Photo Flight International 1972

FLIGHT INTERNATIONAL 20 APRIL 1972

Hanover Show guide

FLIGHT

INTERNATIONAL

'Flight' team test 2 : Messerschmitt-B-B Monsun

Battersea Heliport 1972

Chris de Vere acknowledging his photographer from the rear of his Air & Space 18a Autogiro G-BALB at Battersea Heliport, possibly a first from Biggin Hill. I had a lot of time for Chris due to his enthusiasm for aviation and his willingness to share in conversation. There were others at Biggin and increasing in numbers, that were so far up they own undercarriage in their attempt to make one feel the under-dog. This plastic superior attitude failed to impress me having been around long enough to ignore such Apsole's. Not all these new types had money, those that did were living a dream world far from reality creating new clubs and small charter companies earning the rank of a "Four Tenner". I have no idea who came up with this rank but it suited so many of the new arrivals on Biggin. Possibly intoxicated by its history, but with Rolls or Bentley and cheque books flashed as if they were waste paper they courted failure. Time would tell the full and sad story of those newly painted aircraft fleets, matching limo's and attractive females in pencil skirts as receptionists, all disappearing within a year and the dreamer catching the 410 bus back to Bromley.

I would have loved to have flown Gypsy Moth G-ABYA that was hangared at Coby's, ex Surrey and Kent hangar as it was known for many years.

Doug Gilbert and friend with G-ABYA

DH60G Gypsy Moth serial number 1906 had been originally purchased by a Mr. Maldon Harley in 1932. On his death, March 1966, he entrusted this machine to the Shuttleworth Collection. One of the later owners was listed as Woodley which I took to be Mike Woodley of Aces High that were based at North Weald. Unfortunately this beautiful aircraft was lost on the 21st May 1972 at the Air Fair. Both pilot, Ian Hay, and passenger, Susie Scrivener, survived the impact ending in the trees on the far side of the Main Road close to the end of 03 runway. Susie suffered facial injury but after extensive surgery she made a full recovery. In 2003 this machine was a project for the Channel Four Salvage Squad and was completely rebuilt.

Sad news for our airport on the 15th June 1972. Bromley Council agreed to purchase most of Biggin Hill Airport from the M.o.D. The deal being completed during 1974. Price paid £480.000. I remember walking across the apron talking with Barry Wheeler after a few pints in the Flairavia bar, his final comment was: *"It's all over Joe."*

Chapter Fourteen

I shall never forget Barry's statement, he was so right. Once Bromley Council took over Biggin Hill from Orpington, due to boundary changes, things started going downhill. Biggin Hill Valley would change its colouring from green to concrete grey. Truly sad to see so many trees lost as land with a single dwelling was now authorised for 4, 6 or as many dwellings as they could squeeze on these 1918 sites. What was going to happen to our historic airfield now these morons would have control? Let's be perfectly honest Bromley Council had the problem disposing of rubbish, so what chance did they have running and organising an active aviation facility with more movements than London Heathrow Airport. One good thing however, the take over from M.o.D. would not take place for another two years.

Flying Airtourer G-AZHI over South East London one pleasant Saturday afternoon with a friend the cock-pit started to fill with a small amount of smoke.
"This happen often Joe?." Asked my friend.
"Only on bank holidays." I replied.
I immediately checked the instrument panel at the same time opening and closing the throttle, all seemed normal but the smoke became thick encouraging me to reach for the canopy lever. Opening the canopy the smoke cleared instantly but continued to seep from the instrument panel. I called Biggin.
"Biggin Tower this is Golf-Alfa-Zulu-Hotel- India do you read."
All I received in my head set reminded me of a famous breakfast cereal, smack crackle and pop. Should I have to put the aircraft down I couldn't be in a better place as the site of Blackheath Common was on the nose reassuring me I could possible get a pint in the Sun in the Sand pub.
"Biggin Tower this is Golf-Alfa-Zulu-Hotel-India do you read."
The same continual sound from my head set, the fact the engine was running normally gave me the confidence we had a radio fire. I turned the aircraft back home bound informing my puzzled passenger of my intentions.
"Sorry Phil I have to get back to Biggin now."

Joining the busy Saturday afternoon traffic was no problem as I made a direct approach for runway 23, I had no wish to join the circuit if my luck ran out. Parking the aircraft we walked back to the club filling out the flight sheet stating the aircraft was unserviceable due to radio fire. I never heard another thing. I did phone the tower apologising for my non radio arrival. Truly, I think they had little idea I had arrived.

Chapter Fourteen

I had little to do with Biggin during the remainder of 1972 as my position with Vickers took on a 7 day week trying to complete the tasks set before the office. Stock taking had gone from once a year to twice making the day-today duties challenging. Keeping the factory at Margate stocked and the sundries warehouse at Orpington satisfied plus all the out of dated costing methods we had to work with made for long hours. Where was the computer that the boss had boasted about.

My policy was for suppliers representative visits to be by appointment only. However, no representative was to be sent away without being seen by me or by one of the staff should we be available. This policy was questioned, can you believe it, by our sales office as a waste of my office time. My reply was if a representative took the trouble of calling it was only correct to give them time to promote their products and services. On one occasion I did see a cold caller from a plastic moulding company that produced plastic sinks. We were in the process of modernising the gentlemen's room on the factory floor and in need of 6 new sinks. The salesperson went into his spiel regarding the sink, placed it inverted on my office floor and then proceeded to jump up and down on its base. There followed the most amazing crack as his pride and joy burst into 100 pieces. Red faced and stuttering like an old Ford he apologised stating this had never happened before.

"Would you care for tea?" I asked.

"Thank you, two sugars please." He replied wiping his brow of sweat.

After taking tea I had the factory manager inspect the remains of the sink and explained the reason for the damage. He laughed and agreed the sink was suitable for his needs. The very embarrassed representative left with the remains of his sink and an order for 6 complete units.

I had the opportunity to visit our Dutch manufacturing unit based in the small town of Amersfoot. Here they produced litho plates and chemicals using the most antiquated equipment I had ever seen, All be it in small quantities but with profit margins that were the envy of the main production team in the UK.

We had many problems with our Italian supplier of graphic machinery who ignored our requests for credit notes for returned units. No way would they negotiate by correspondence. Needing a break I received permission to drive down and incorporate the visit with a weeks holiday in Monte Carlo. After my call at their factory we received all outstanding credits on my return.

The summer of 1973 was a little sad as both Gwyn Russell and Barry Wheeler had moved on. Gwyn, still in the R.A.F., was posted north, and Barry was now a family man with young children so financing flying was not his first priority. I did fly with other friends in various aircraft as P2, I didn't worry about building up flying hours as my dream of becoming an assistant instructor had long vanished.

Photo: © Pilots Pals

Biggin Hill Air Fair 1973

Gary, our 16 month old son with Brendan O'Brien during the show that would see the new Rothmans Aerobatic Teams aircraft. 4 Pitts S-2A Specials.

The 1973 oil crises started in October when Arab oil producing countries proclaimed an oil embargo in response to America's decision to re-supply Israeli military during the Yom Kippur War that ended in March 1974. With supplies disrupted prices increased affecting the entire Western industrial world. Keeping up with the demand of our factories was a huge challenge, thank goodness I had a great relationship with my main suppliers of oil based products, hydrocarbons and ketons being just two of our bulk products required to keep the chemical factory ticking over . Again it was the old problem of storage for the bulk deliveries and often had to request our suppliers to deliver within one hour.

Chapter Fourteen

John Jackson the chemist and factory manager together with his team were forced to juggle day-today production, planning was almost impossible as all packaging containers were scarce. With so many purchase requisitions I was forced to buy from agents rather than the main manufactures and pay inflated prices, better we paid the agents price than allowing the chemical production come to a halt. Almost everything was is short supply and increasing in cost, a buyers worst nightmare and keeping track of prices for costing was a daily chore. The company was large users of Gum Arabic both for production and for resale with a requirement of 500 tonnes, small compared with other users of this natural product. The specification for our use was extremely high with the best gum coming from the Kordofan area of Sudan. The price increased from £495.00 to £ 5000.00 per tonne in a month always provided the supplier could deliver. This Gum Arabic crises had nothing to do with the oil situation but must have had an influence with the hiking of the price to this all time high. Our gum agents said the lack of rain across the Sudan had led to a crop failure. Our production director instructed me to fly to the Sudan when possible together with John Jackson to investigate for ourselves the real reason for this shortage and extremely high price.

The company secretary arranged for us to travel with B.O.A.C., London to Khartoum, departing at midnight for a 6 hours flight. I have had a dislike for this organisation since one of their advertisements said, and I quote, *"FLY BRITISH"* yet it depicted a Boeing 707. However, after a five star meal coupled by a few bottles of red wine my partner, only known to me as a very strict disciplinarian understandable in view of his responsibilities, started to question me on our travel arrangements.

"Hotel booked Joe?"

"Of course John."

"Have you checked the taxi situation here?"

"Available 24 hours, no problem."

"Internal flights and over land vehicles available?"

"All available, bookings in Khartoum."

"Have you checked the Camel availability and their water days?"

"Camels, water days, I don't understand John."

"Camels, should we have to track across the desert using Camels are you aware on the watering procedure on a 5 days trip if you get a 4 day camel."

"No John."

I was feeling a little peed off by his questions that were pointless.

Chapter Fourteen

"I left all arrangement to you, and you have failed to research all means of transport, most important the Camel watering procedure, let me explain".

He continued.

"Before leaving for your journey you take the Camel to the water hole, just as he starts to take his head out of the water having filled up clap his knackers with the two bricks provided, he'll take on an extra days water but watch your thumbs."

I was in pain laughing, John of all people, what happened to that strict boss of the chemical facility that I had a great respect for but now seeing a different person, our ten day visit was hilarious.

9th December 1973 we left Heathrow in a frost covered VC10 around mid-night and I fell into a deep sleep possibly the result of the red wine and the warmth of the cabin. I awoke at 5 am with the most painful dry throat, attracted the attention of a stewardess and asked for a glass of water.

"Can't you wait, breakfast will be served in 15 minutes."

"No, I can't wait." I replied thinking of the Camels knackers.

Water, I needed some fluid to rid myself of this discomfort, Christ where is that woman I thought, suddenly she appeared with a glass of orange, not that I was worried of the contents of the container as I gulped the liquid to ease my thirst. This unfortunate situation only increased my dislike for this organisation swearing I would do my best never to use them for future travel.

Having landed at Khartoum, cleared customs and collected our luggage the priority was to obtain some local currency, not available in the UK. The taxi rank at the airport was very much the same as all airports only Khartoum taxis were 1960's Hillman Minxes with a free air flow system, the only glass being the windscreen fitted to protect the driver's eyes. The body work had a mallet finish complemented with areas of rust. Our driver loaded the boot with our luggage ensured that the rubber strap was tight and secure and then I gave him orders to take us to the nearest bank. He indicated that we should board his vehicle and we both jumped in what looked like a wreck. The engine started giving me thoughts of two metal skeletons making love on a cast iron park bench, at this point I think he let the clutch out when the taxi launched itself into the air then only to be forced against the front seats as he applied the brakes, a large cloud of dust went drifting down the road as all became very quiet, he jumped out opening my door stating.

"Bank sir." The bank entrance was next door to the airport exit.

We did experience some hostility from the Sudan authorities, they tried to prevent us travelling to the Acacia tree orchards that were one hours flying south of Khartoum. Having travelled thousands of miles to find the answers my superiors wanted, I was not prepared to be shoved off by some Sudanese bureaucrat, after all, we were the customer. My persistence and use of some pure English bullshit eventually convinced the Sudan Airways clerk to allow me to purchase two day return air tickets to El Obeid. A few days later we were back at Khartoum Airport boarding a Fokker F-27, Friendship, together with 20 or so other passengers.

The Sudanese Gum Company had arranged for us to be collected at El Obeid airport and taken to the area manager's office by Land Rover. The driver looked like a lost Aborigine soldier in Australian khaki uniform. Circa 1915, complete with the Oz hat. We drove through the small village into a sparse area containing one large shed. Being shown through what resembled a door I was gob smacked to be greeted by a very tall Sudanese gentleman immaculately dressed in Army uniform

"Hello chaps, welcome to El Obeid." He said in Queen's English.

"Good morning Sir, Sandhurst." I asked.

"Yes, did all my early days there, far better than this tour."

Photo: © Pilots Pals

This visit gave us the true situation of the Sudanese problem. The lack of rain across the Sudan had not affected the crop but had dried up the watering holes thus preventing the picking boys from travelling around in the vast areas. This photograph shows the tool used (a) for piercing the tree allowing the gum to ooze out and harden in the sun and (b) for then cutting the gum off the tree trunks. The saying "Stuck up a gum tree" has little to do with the gum but refers to the trees thin branches that resemble Velcro. On our departure the well spoken Army Officer informed us that we had been followed by the Sudanese secret police all day. Interesting.

Sudan's Miracle Commodity.

Arabic translated means = Pure, Translucent.

Gum Arabic

Acacia trees grow throughout Africa and too on the Indian subcontinent. Most of the world's gum, however, comes from Sudan, where a thick belt of Acacia trees stretches from one side of the country to the other.

Gum Arabic is a natural emulsifier, which means that it can keep together substances which normally would not mix. Gum users include the Cosmetic. Pharmaceutical, Food, Soft Drinks and Printing industries. Another well known use is in lickable adhesives for postage stamps and envelopes. One of natures natural gifts to all humanity. The Sudanese gum is the finest quality produced in the world and demands the best price. Other African products are darker in colour, are not as pure and are used in a very different market such a pet foods.

The last evening in Sudan we ate in the Grand Hotel on the Blue Nile having a small glimpse of the old Khartoum. I was convinced that the hotel, its staff and the equipment, had not seen a change since Lord Kitchener of Khartoum had his last meeting there back in 1902. It was in the early 1950's that my mischievous friend Douglas Gilbert had sat in this very hotel, no doubt sipping a large whisky and planning his next exploit to earn a crust. It was wonderful to witness the Victorian splendour and experience, probably for the only time in my life, such a true step back in time.

On my return to England western gum buyers, including some very big names in the industry, organised a meeting at the Dorchester Hotel, London. A French company headed the meeting and suggested that we pool our requirements and procure through a single channel via France thus guaranteeing requirements. Now having first-hand knowledge of the true situation of supply I had my doubts regarding our French mates and what lay behind their proposal. Later in life I learned that our French mates had found a method of producing 'Sudan Kordofan' quality gum in powder form from lower quality gums, clever buggers.

Chapter 15

Going into 1974 with continuing long hours at work I had even more problems with the shortages, the oil crisis was hurting most companies and individuals. I remember aviation fuel being a problem but never affecting the small amount of time I spent flying at Biggin Hill. The most important moment in this year would be an addition to our family coupled with having no money worries, a good feeling.

Joseph J. Merchant 2011

Once the oil embargo was lifted matters started to return to normal except for the hours required to satisfy my company. We had the most amazing cooperation from our main suppliers, allowing the sites to keep up and running. The company showed its appreciation to me with several salary increases and a company car; but the hours were demanding with a stock take now every quarter. The profits we made were staggering, increasing each year by another million. Back to Biggin Hill.

Photo: © Via Garry Studd

Garry Studd with Dragon Rapide 4R-AA1

Another great character who learnt to fly with Mick Ronayne at Flairavia in 1969/70 was Garry who, as he puts it.
"Just scraped through my PPL within a couple of weeks of becoming 17."
Garry went on to become an instructor for Flairavia and later acted as C.F.I. for both Biggin Hill Flying School and Surrey & Kent Flying Club. The above image was taken on the 10th March 1974 the day Garry landed at Biggin Hill after ferrying this Rapide from Sri Lanka. The signatures on the fuselage were collected from well wishers during his return flight. I was amazed to see Douglas Gilbert had added his name to the many. Garry went on to fly Doves and Herons with Fairflight and survived his first Atlantic ferry job to Winnipeg with "Uncle Bill Webb"

Chapter Fifteen

"Uncle Bill Webb"

Uncle Bill Webb as most of us knew him was 100% aviation. Ex R.A.F. served in South Africa during WW II as a Technical Officer. After the war he set up business at Croydon Airport purchasing Tiger Moths from the M.o.D. In 1959 he moved to Biggin Hill when Croydon closed. Doug Gilbert delivered several of Bill's Tigers to various airstrips around England but stopping en rout to sell joy rides to the locals for 5 shillings a head. Bill soon found out why Douglas was always late on delivery and that put an end to Doug's get rich quick venture.

Photo: © Garry Studd

28th April 1974 at Queen Mary's Hospital, Sidcup my wife gave us another son and agreed he should be named after our great friend Roy Sanders (P.1.G). The happiness both boys gave me was truly priceless, the simple things like a walk in the park with our dog Brandy was great fun. I believe this was one of the most valuable times of my life and deeply regret the times I was unable to be with them for whatever reason. Preparation for a visit to Biggin Hill at week-ends was more like going on holiday considering the amount of goodies needed for two young boys plus dog on a day out. Leaving the airport before the bars got going was heart-breaking but that was the price we both paid for our family.

Photo: © Via ADI

Ormond Haydon-Baillie

This ex Royal Canadian Air Force instructor with his "Black Knight" image brought a little glamour into both aviation and Biggin Hill during the 1974 Air Fair. I never had the opportunity to meet him but admired his flying ability and aircraft. He lost his life flying Mustang P51-D I-BILL, on 3rd July 1977. A pilot with many friends around the world winning the respect of all that had the opportunity to work with him.

197

"The Black Knight"

The distinctive paint scheme of Haydon-Baillie's T33 Silver Star G-OAHB became an overnight success with the pilots at Biggin Hill, he was a very special pilot with a flair for aviation entertainment.

Haydon-Baillie's Sea Fury G-AGHB at Biggin Hill 17th May 1974

Bill Webb - Graham Jackson
August 1974

This photograph was taken just before
the departure of a ferry flight to Canada
shows one of the many D.H. Doves and
Herons Bill flew for export around the
world.

He was a very special man willing to
give opportunities to our younger pilots
essential for their future careers.

Photo: © Garry Studd

End of the runway   Photo: © Dave Manghan

This Bristol 175 Britannia 312 ex Air Spain EC-BFJ comes to a unhappy
end on the East apron where so many other aircraft were broken up during
the 1970's. Not sure who had this contact but it seems to stop in the 1980's.

Greenham Common was our meeting point for the 1974 International Air Tattoo. Barry Wheeler (Scoop) and I arranged to meet Roy Sanders (P.1.G) at a small B & B just outside the airfield. It being Friday afternoon most of the aircraft were already assembled and Roy suggested we take a look around to get some good photos before the masses arriving the next day.

"Do you have V.I.P. Tickets." I asked him.

"Don't need 'em, just follow my instructions and all will be well. Both of you sit in the back of my car, I will drive." He replied.

Roy who was wearing his green flying jacket half covered in aviation badges proceeded to drive straight for the main entrance at some speed throwing up salutes to all and sundry. We were in the security area of Greenham Common heading for yet another barrier that lifted as Roy produced more of his well worn American salutes. Barry and I looked at one another and burst into uncontrollable laughter as we continued to head for the many static aircraft parked on the other side of the base.

Roy calmly parked the car among the fighters, looked at us with that contented smile and said.

"Should get some good scoops Barry, take your time."

Barry had his trusted 35 mm camera ready to do his best with this unique opportunity. At some distance I saw a Vulcan what appeared to be making an approach heading for the lines of fighter. I screamed to Barry.

"Scoop."

Pointing in the direction of the on coming Vulcan I took a few shots with my 35mm then having a great sight as the aircraft opened up to give us the view of the typical Vulcan climb out feeling the vibrations through the hard stand concrete. Barry and Roy wandered off to get as many shots as possible leaving me to enjoy the sunshine and experience the strange feeling of loneliness, knowing if we were caught they would throw away the keys.

The sudden appearance of a American Military Policeman walking toward me was, to say the least, somewhat a worrying moment particularly as I had lost sight of both Roy and Barry. As he was still some distance away I came up with an idea but it would be a challenge to convince the police officer I was a British astronaut visiting for the week-end. He was carrying an automatic weapon in the semi ready position and said.

"Your pass sir?"

My reply was weak, pathetic and stupid coming straight out of the Goons.

"I don't need one"

Instantly he saluted and replied.

"Thank you sir, have a nice day."

I never had a chance to see if he would swallow the astronaut story so, being a little relieved and concerned that he may have had time to think about my reply I rushed to find my friends. We drove off the airfield as quickly as we had arrived with Roy continuing to throw those silly salutes to anyone in uniform. Time for a pint and talk of our unauthorised visit and plan the rest of the week-end.

"What shall we do this evening? Asked Roy adding *"I understand there's a bash at the Officer Mess tonight, shall we go?"*

. Barry burst out laughing at the suggestion we should attend the mess party.

"Roy, are you completely out of your tiny mind." I said.

"Easy," replied Roy. *"When we get to the entrance I will lead and then turn to you Joe and ask for the tickets I gave you earlier. Then you turn to Barry and ask for the tickets you passed to him earlier. Barry will then deny all knowledge of the tickets."*

"You are completely out of your box Roy but I love it." I remarked

That evening it was raining heavily, we parked the car and ran to the Officers Mess entrance and as planned we all played our part in this very dramatic scene of panic over the lost tickets. Believe it or not.

"Come on sir, move on, move on please." Said the door Sergeant.

We spent the evening with the crews getting rather inebriated singing songs with one of the Arrows playing the piano. What a party.

Photo: © Barry Wheeler

50 Sqn. Avro Vulcan B.2 XM597

597 was flown into and retired at East Fortune, Scotland April 1984

Gloster Meteor NF11 (TT20) WD592

Parked at Biggin Hill January 1975 this NF11 served with the R.A.F. Prior to conversion to a TT20 for the Royal Navy. Note the roundels and the wording "Royal Navy" on the rear of the fuselage have been painted over indicating it had been taken out of service but not yet carrying any registration. It was sold to Letcher & Associates 18th June registered N94749. Little is known of this machine once in the U.S.A. other than it was filmed at Chino for the Wonder Woman episode "The Feminum Mystique" in 1976. 1988 ownership passed to Al Hansen and Ascher Ward. In 1994 it was donated to Edwards Air Force Base Flight Test Museum at Mojave, California. The AEC London bus, RT9229, was owned by Robin Phillips who gave his many friends a ride just for the fun of it. For a while there were two of these parked on Biggin Hill the other belonged to "Jock" Maitland and was used during the Air Fairs for visitors joy rides to the aircraft static area, also giving photographers an unique opportunity.

The 1975 Air Fair saw the introduction of a B17. This ex USAF aircraft was sold to France in 1954 for survey work and registered as F-BGSR. Then obtained by businessman Ted White, registered N17TE, in March 1975 christened "Sally B". Elly Sallingboe and her dedicated team of supporters have achieved remarkable results keeping her in the air for so many years ensuring future generations have the opportunity to witness what their forefathers flew and fought in during WW II. Became G-BEDF 1976.

Alan Humphreys plus Rolls-Royce with Ted White.

There were some beautiful vehicles owned by the many pilots at Biggin Hill one in particular was the hand built one off John Dodd's "The Beast" This amazing machine was fitted with the Merlin engine plus Rolls-Royce radiator grille, badges and the "Spirit of Ecstasy" mascot, none of which were authorised by the manufacturers. In 1974 "The Beast" was brought to the attention of Rolls-Royce, who took John to court after he refused to remove their radiator grille, badges and mascot. After appearing in court nine times and given a six months jail sentence for contempt of court, the Rolls-Royce trademark features were removed and the grille was replaced with one bearing Dodd's "JD" initials. The contempt of court incident made national news. The judge making reference to John's attitude of that of a cavalier, not being beaten John turned out the following day in a riding outfit on the back of a horse that he rode up to the court entrance. In my book John and his family were one of the greats of Biggin Hill, he is a genuine human and a brilliant engineer for the worlds auto gear box problems.

The many stories that surround John Dodd would not only make entertaining reading but could possibly turn the heads of the film makers throughout the world.

John Dodd's "The Beast"

Once listed in the Guinness Book of Records as the world's most powerful road car "The Beast" has used two different fibreglass bodies during its life; the first was destroyed in a fire. John being John rebuilt the engine and commissioned a new body. Today both John and the car reside in Spain, occasionally appearing at automotive shows. He is very similar to his car, a one off and also a competent pilot. The Hunter G-HUNT in Mike Carlton's collection was one of the first ex Danish Air Force of its type to have a civilian registration rebuilt by engineer Eric Haywood.. During 1987 it was sold to the U.S.A.

Biggin Hill Airport was now in the hands of Bromley Council and one of the first things they did was to start asset stripping the south camp by selling off 10% to produce the industrial estate area. The only other presence of authority was the erection of a security box on the south camp. This unfortunately was damaged when Doug Gilbert accidentally reversed into it six times with a borrowed lorry. It was never replaced.

I do remember the Council making their first official visit with tea and buns. I never knew the name of the councillor who made the speech saying.
"What a pleasure it was to visit the Biggin Hill Conning Tower."
His mind obviously thinking of the financial gain that would be adding to the Council's pot. The only conning tower was in the town hall at Bromley.

I always had a haunting feeling when visiting our chapel. If I was truthful my feeling would go out to the boys and girls we lost, so many and such a waste. Understanding their commitment made a chill run through my body. Simply thinking of what must have been uncontrollable terror and yet they stayed by their post completing their duty. Think of them too long and I was sad so best I would make my visits short and sweet always signing the book and placing a few bob in the tin. I have to be honest again and add I don't think I ever wanted to discuss this deep emotion with others, it is far too deep turning to anger.

St. Georges Chapel of Remembrance R.A.F. Biggin Hill

The Chapel Green   Photo: © Pilots Pals

Janice, my wife, with our boys, Gary and Roy. This would have been a visit on a Sunday, possibly too early for the club to be open. The Spitfire was SL674 one of the two gate guardians, its partner was Hurricane IIcb LF739.

The Royal Air Force with its Aircrew Selection Centre at Biggin Hill seemed too be the right place, not to far from London and what a better place to have young men and women start their careers at this historic R.A.F. Station.

The last Battle of Britain "Open Day" at R.A.F. Biggin Hill
September 1976

Photos: © Norman Rivett

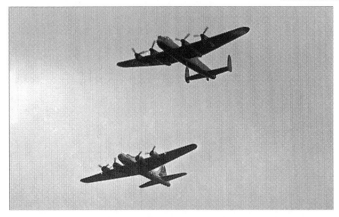

A rare formation sight - "Sally B" and the R.A.F. Lancaster

The R.A.F. Biggin Hill Air Commodore inspecting Sportair's Stampe SV4B G-AZSA ex Belgium Air Force V-61 this became the pride and joy of the humorous Keith Faulkner for over 20 years. As for many other R.A.F. bases it was a sad time for Biggin Hill losing the Battle of Britain day, at least we had "Jock" Maitland providing us with the successful annual Air Fair.

Chapter Fifteen

The social scene had changed, long gone were the days when the south east was the main flying club area; now most had closed or moved to the south camp joining KingAir Flying Club, Flairavia and Biggin Hill Flying Club each having a far better view of the airfield plus the added bonus of being close to the airport entrance, giving a better chance of grabbing new clients for training or joy flights. Richard Elles, Chief Flying Instructor, and Pam his wife were running the Biggin Hill Flying Club owned then by the Gold brothers, David and Ralph. Their building was one of the original R.A.F. store sheds, built with a high quantity of asbestos, but by comparison with the old clubs it was large and had the luxury of both ladies and gent toilets. The large kitchen provided Sunday lunches prepared by Pam Elles and her team.

My social visits were now restricted due to my work and to family commitments, but by organising a baby sitter we could attend a few parties at the Biggin Hill Flying Club. There I met John Willis who was, at that time, running the disco for the evening entertainment. More of Roy Sanders (P.1.G) miming to Shirley Bassey and Victor Borge. He was so enthusiastic and his performances proved his ability to study each of his subjects in minute detail, a great success with the many members.

During a rare Saturday visit I saw that King Air Flying Club were operating a Chipmunk. Having the finance I decided to get a check out and get back to my old ways by flying a real aircraft. In their office I asked for details and price for their Chipmunk. A young man, wearing a white shirt with the bullshit stripes, immediately assailed me with the complications of tail wheeled aircraft without giving me the opportunity to tell of my experience. I listened thinking I wonder if he had been breast fed and stayed on to long. I'd had enough of his bullshit and said;

"Excuse me young man, I may have not flown for two years but I'm sure that since then the world of aviation has not produced a new thousand page instructional manual on flying. Price per hour please."
He came back with questions.
"What have you flown and with whom?" "When did you last fly P1?"
I started to get annoyed as I had my log book in my hand.
"How many hours do you have as P1?"
At this point I just looked him in the eye, allowed him to babble on saying.
"You will need a G.F.T. (General Flight Test) after spending time in the circuit, stalling and spinning.

Chapter Fifteen

"My I take this opportunity to say goodbye." I said and walked out.

My flying days were well and truly over, I had become a "has been that never was." I'd had a great time flying great aircraft together with some wonderful people in an environment that was fast becoming as rare a rocking horse shit. In reality flying had become a serious matter with everything to be done by the book! You had to ask the control tower if you wanted to move an aircraft from A to B. Christ what happened to looking out of the cockpit. The circuit became controlled increasing the time it took to complete a single circuit turning finals at South Bromley. I disliked the modern flying Biggin Hill. Gone forever knocking seven colours of sugar out of the clubs with low flying or completing a few basic aerobatic manoeuvres after closing time, or having ones own way on Boxing day. As my good friend Barry Wheeler had said.

"It's all over Joe."

The social life now improved at the Biggin Hill Flying Club, producing the environment that I loved and life once again became more enjoyable. I met new people; some well known in the air show circuit flying a collection of war birds. Chris Bevan flying Spitfires, Keith Sissons the captain of Ted White's B17 "Sally B" to name a couple. The shy and well liked aviation photographer Norman Rivett who has been a very important part of this publication captured high quality photographs of the early days of civilian flying at Biggin Hill Airport.

Another commercial company using Biggin Hill during the 70's was Robertson Foods Ltd. The much loved logo proudly displayed on the fin and engine cowlings of their Piper PA-31 350 Navajo Chieftain. How times have changed. G-OLLY photographed at Manchester International Airport.

Photo: © Andy Kennaugh

Our boys Roy & Gary

What parents couldn't be proud of their children. Biggin Hill Airport was an important part of their youth most week-ends spent meeting new and old friends. I carried this photo for many years to remind me of better times.

Chapter Fifteen

Chapter 16

Both our boys were growing up and life became a little easier with our visits to Biggin Hill. Instead of their nappies and food the load became their bikes and, of course, plasters since just as their Father fell off horses so they fell off their bikes. The social life at Biggin would have a new venue allowing us to make new friends. My employment would see a change, a change that would not be to the benefit of the company but the individuals. The accountants were breeding like rabbits and too the Public Relations team. Time to move.

Joseph J. Merchant 2011

Miles M.3A Falcon Major G-AEEG   Photo:© Norman Rivett

This excellent air to air photograph shows G-AEEG over West Camp 19th March 1977 flown by Ian Dalziel (Doc). Manufactured by Philips & Powis in 1936 and sold to Sweden as SE-AFN. The Swedish Air Force impressed it in 1939 as Fv7001. At the end of hostilities it returned to its original registration. Imported back to England 1962 and restored in 1963. In 1979 it became the oldest aircraft to win the Kings Cup Air Race.

The ex M.I.T. married quarters Vincent Square can be clearly seen under the port wing. The lower left area, also M.o.D. was redeveloped by 2004 with a promise of a Museum. Did you see that pig fly over?

Chapter Sixteen

We continued to enjoy our week-ends at the Biggin Hill Flying Club taking full advantage of Pam Elles' lunch time menus. This made my wife's life a lot easier by not having to worry about cooking the Sunday roast. Pam's husband, Richard Elles, was the Chief Flying Instructor until the club was sold to Tree Haven Trust in 1977. They had ideas of building an hotel, a project that never materialised like so many before. I had seen plans and models for the development that resembled Las Vegas in the past but nothing ever happened. I bet a council were involved in their failure.

I believe it was on a Saturday afternoon, while sitting outside the club, when I heard what sounded like a formation of miss firing tractors. It was the arrival of a West Essex Flying Club Rollason Condor, G-AWFN, piloted by Tony Bebrough with young Billy Robinson as passenger. Both were looking a slightly discoloured shade of grey reinforced by a plastic smile. After shutting the aircraft down both climbed out vibrating like a couple of puppets to tell their story of a broken prop. On inspection the engine mounts had only just held, thus saving both their lives. Tony, the pilot, was another great Biggin Hill character always ready for a good time, I cannot remember Tony not having a smile. Young Billy, only 15, helped out in the original Tower after school and at week-ends proving his enthusiasm for aviation. He became one of the dedicated team working in the control tower and was elevated to Chief Air Traffic Controller in 2008. Known to many as a hard working social addict Billy spent many years working with "Jock" Maitland and later Colin Hitchens on the Biggin Hill Air Fair. He was an essential member of the organising team for this successful annual international event. I'm convinced if you cut Billy in half you would find the words "Biggin Hill" running from head to toe as in a stick of sweet rock. I was the lucky one for Billy and his wife Sandra became lifelong friends.

Understanding the management of Biggin Hill it came as no surprise to me the contract for the air show was cancelled a week after the 2010 show. A very sad day for Biggin Hill Airport, the local residents and too the many thousands of aviation enthusiast that attended the event each year.

Back at work the challenge became even greater with the expansion of the company and their products. Meeting the demands of the various manufacturing units with sundries, chemicals and machinery stocks was demanding on my loyal staff. The more our office achieved it seemed the more demands and responsibilities came our way. Back to Biggin.

Although there were many other bars on the airport a new watering hole was created by Mark Campbell out of the closure of Flairavia Flying Club . He obtained the liquor licence under the pretence of "The Private Owners Club". It was the smallest bar on Biggin christened "Swordfish". I should imagine named after the Royal Navy Memorial Flight aircraft and the crews that frequented it during their air show appearance. It was during one of their shows that I met Pete Sheppard one Navy pilot who flew the Sea Fury. I remember him as a real Navy type complete with beard and the spirit and enthusiasm of a jolly pirate. Both ground and aircrew were great fun, the members enjoying the banter that came with every pint. Mark Campbell and Sue, his wife, did a great job looking after their guests over the four day event.

The 1977 show was marred by the collision between a sight seeing helicopter on lift off with a landing Tiger Moth, sadly 5 persons in the helicopter lost their lives. The Tigers undercarriage was sheared off but it landed without injuries to its crew. Extensive damage was caused to several parked aircraft.

Trojan T-28 N99160   Photo: © Peter Pain

4 of these ex Congolese and Zaire Air Force aircraft were imported from the Congo, 3 make it to Biggin Hill the forth N-99153 crashed in Limoges, France on the 14th December 1977. I did have the opportunity to take air to air photos from Mike Dunkley's Harvard of one of the remaining 3 aircraft. Handing the roll of film 35mm to an aviation magazine. I never received a

copy for myself although my picture was used as a centrefold and my copy of that has disappeared. Unfortunately the civilian buyers of these aircraft were unaware of the small print on the original sales agreement that stated, "*Aircraft must to be returned to the United State to be demilitarised*". Thus putting a sad end to this venture. The fuselage of N99153, that crashed in France, is now on display at the Norfolk and Suffolk Aviation Museum.

My career with Algraphy had to take first place, my salary providing the necessary finance for our family holidays in Spain and for the private education at the local Catholic school in Sidcup for our sons. This training school must have been the last from the Victorian period with discipline that could bring tears to a Sergeant Majors eyes. To give you an idea of their strict demands on the children, bearing in mind parents were informed of the Sisters methods before the child being delivered on its first day. One nasty little boy who refused to sit down was tied to his chair for the entire morning lessons. Gary, our son, who witnessed the entire saga told us little nasty boy had a very sore throat and was never seen again obviously returning home possible taking it out of Mum and Dad who failed to apply the same discipline. Both Gary and Roy loved the Sisters who paid great attention to all the children winning their respect. This affection reminded me of my days with the cadets, the respect I had for our NCO's who made us a cohesive unit and proud to be a part of a team. Discipline has long gone from schools turning the tables on authority. I have seen children kicking their Mothers in the shins using the F word, a sad story of reality of our modern world. If the child acts in this way, the chances are the parents are the inadequate teachers.

Dusty" Taylor the export sales manager for Algraphy had four beautiful apartments in Torredembarra, about 78 kilometres south of Barcelona and hired them out to friends very cheaply. For many years we travelled down by car, the journey taking around 28 hours through France to sunny Spain. Torredembarra, like most of the coast line in Spain was idyllic. One block of apartments and one 1930's hotel on a five mile empty beach with the most picturesque fishing village in the centre. It was stunning and convenient albeit you had to drive from the beach to the small village inland to use the local restaurants and bars. Both boys enjoyed their limited freedom making new friends every year, swimming becoming second nature. I came across the famous Torres wines, brandy and liqueurs centre in Villa Franca, visits to their distillery made my holidays. I drink Torres to this day.

The installation of a new computer costing system at Algraphy required that our office run in parallel with the accounts office for more than two years. This to ensure the complete loading of formulae for each manufactured product. Continuously updating was the success of this programme; to the advantage of our sales department and also the quarterly stock take eased the pressure on my staff. Our small accounts department at Orpington was then transferred to Leeds making it clear to me that my days were coming to an end. Although meetings with the new management were held with the possibility of transferring me and the office to Leeds I felt them to be both untrustworthy and distasteful. I was not keen on their wasteful procedures; bloody memos arriving meaning sweet sod all and always a copy to my boss. I shall never forget receiving a computer print out of our raw materials with a memo requesting I give a two year forecast of future markets. Not bothering to look at each product I simply entered anything between 2% and 7% and completed this silly request in a couple of days. Remember "Bullshit baffles Brains". There is not a human that could forecast the petrochemicals market for the next 6 months let alone 2 years as requested. Silly buggers .I would put money on it that all my guess work was never used or even looked at. It was typical of employees that don't have enough to do so they create paperwork for some busy sod like me to prove they have achieved something, sod all.

I was not prepared to move to Leeds taking my family away from the environment of Biggin Hill and being honest with myself I knew only too well I was not qualified for the job. The amount of money our office had saved the company was staggering plus the fact that manufacturing units that never came to a halt due to the chase procedure applied to all purchases. Our relations with the main suppliers of petrochemicals was a very healthy one, my purchasing policy of "Respect the Rep" really did pay off. I was extremely proud of my staff and their achievements but later in life realising how stupid I had been not to line my own pockets making my later life a lot easier.

Knowing my time with Howson Algraphy, as it became, would soon end and longing to work for myself I started inventing new gadgets. All my experience at W.F. Stanley came into action having the know how with machine tools. The first invention was a security alarm for windows, doors or your pocket. It fired on demand spraying the intruder with a dye making the most uncomfortable screaming sound that would deafen any bad boy.

My rough prototype completed I tried to sell the idea only to be told by so many "NO INTEREST". My next project was an idea needing to get in with somebody that could provide finance. Secondary energy was my next goal. I was told by so many of my friends I was nuts thinking up such a stupid idea. As it was a part of my life I feel I should tell the tale of my nutty idea. Secondary energy is the result of spent energy. I came up with the idea of replacing motorway lighting by placing small ducted turbo fans every so often in the central reservation of the motorway. The rush of wind created by passing vehicles powers the fans to light up the motorway ahead, already night clubs in Israel harness power from people dancing, just the movement of their feet creates secondary energy. I gave up all ideas of becoming one of England's great designers working my last few sad weeks at Orpington. I had to say my goodbyes to some of the greatest people I had worked with over the last 10 years. Dennis Beddoes from stock control who felt the same way about the new management as myself. A dedicated employee demoralised by endless instructions with no purpose other than to justify some pen pusher position. My assistant buyer Chris Marshall who's hard work and loyalty to me and the team was always appreciated. I lost touch with Chris in the mid 80's. My last office junior clerk Sue, the ginger lass from Orpington, who's surname has been lost in the years gone by. She became a great friend, one of those females that was enjoyable to talk to, fun to work with and nothing was too much trouble going to great lengths to ensure her duties were completed. It must have been 1985 when returning from a meeting in London I was sitting on a train at Victoria Station when I saw Sue making her way towards the front end of the train, our eyes met making me look away for what reason I have no idea why. It was During my last month I was approached by a rep who was looking for a buyer in the petrochemical world to take up a position in Suffolk. Good salary and perks including resettlement finance. I joined Sign Post Paints in November 1979 taking my 10 years experience with not knowing if my personality would fit the bill. The board of directors were possibly one of the best I had worked with, a breath of fresh air but the middle management I could not handle. Three months later I resigned much to the disappointment of the board. I was now out of work but relieved to be back close to Biggin Hill .

The social life at Biggin took on a new lease of life as more people were using the Mark Campbell's "Swordfish Bar" then run by Valerie Vizer, in my book a smashing woman with a sense of humour that fitted the club. It was here that I met Ralph Scott owner of Express Aviation on the East side

of Biggin Hill. The hanger being the old 600 R.Aux.A.F. H.Q. until 1957.
Ralph, a well respected man whose business was as good as his word. The
aircraft G-BOSS was just one of his sales.

Piper PA.34 - 200T Seneca II G-BOSS Photo: © Richard Dayman

Ralph Scott had control of Express Aviation since 1971 and ran a well
organised, reliable company with a very good reputation around Europe for
sales and servicing. He and his 48 employees were undoubtedly a good
team. I remember Steve Danaher, a junior engineer, remarking on his time
with Express Aviation. *"As, the happiness time in his working life was with
Express under the leadership of Ralph."* The sale of G-BOSS and its
delivery took Ralph to Spain where he, not planned, would put down a
foundation for his future. The sale of Express Aviation to the British Rail
Pension Fund was finalised in 1985 headed by Don Daines. A man that
enjoyed his lunch times. Ralph Scott was to build a new life free of the stress
of running such a large organisation. His adopted the village of El Pinar
giving him new friends in a new environment.

The purchase of 4 ex Portuguese Air Force Harvard's by Mark Campbell,
Ted White, Graham Balls and Stuart Patterson, added the air of excitement
to the "Swordfish Bar", it was a true aviation buzz particularly at week-ends
when the small bar filled with pilots, students and enthusiasts. Although I
had known Mark Campbell for many years since he started his small
business with a bucket and sponge, e.g., the birth of his company Light
Aircraft Valet Service, Mark would go onto form his own charter company
unfortunately the ensuing recession put paid to any further expansion and

he was forced to sell his Harvard. Ted White was the owner of the B-17 'Sally B'. Stuart Patterson operated a charter company, a keen flyer with impeccable manners, he was well liked by all who surrounded him. Graham Balls a private owner, had his business outside aviation. I would have loved to be involved in that team from day one but it was not to be. Having flown only once in the Harvard I found it a great camera ship with its opportunity to open the rear cockpit

"Going flying Doug"   Photo: © Pilots Pals

Our two boys Roy and Gary expecting Douglas Gilbert to say or do something rude as he was so well known for, the boys loved his endless antics. His middle name should have been "Mischief." I did refer to the Guinness before flight, Doug replying in his pure English said.

"Medicinal old boy, purely medicinal."

The aircraft G-BACH owned by Graham Balls registered 25th January 1979. Reregistered reserved G-BXHF June 1980 but never taken up. Reregistered G-VALE 19th September 1980. Sold to the U.S.A. 1985 as N36CA.

I felt insecure not being in employment with a team of people around me to enjoy the challenges put before us. There was the added worry of finance that made my life more uncomfortable. During 1980 I was approached by one of my old suppliers from my Howson Algraphy days to take up a vacancy as petrochemical sales representative for the South of England. Much against my better judgment I joined Samuel Banner Ltd. knowing I would have to face buyers that perhaps had a very different policy towards salesman than my own. "Respect the Rep" would be wishful thinking.

Both our boys were growing up fast requiring more bedroom space for their studies, it was time to move to a larger home with three bedrooms and Sidcup had became too crammed for my liking, it was quicker to walk than attempt to drive your car for shopping. Being on the road 5 days a week with my new employment was not my scene, in fact I hated every day, but it did mean that we could view property at our leisure while the boys were at school. We saw some very beautiful homes but as always way out of our financial reach. Returning to Biggin Hill during the weekend our attention was drawn to a very large notice board next to Squires Timber, The M.o.D. Officers married quarters on the South East side of the airport Dowding Road, Koonowla Close and Crossley Close had been placed on the market through one of the Biggin Hill estate agents. Making enquiries we were told perspective buyers had to bid for each property. After our inspection we placed three bids on three different properties in Koonowla Close winning our first choice number 1. The local estate agents employed a caretaker, Bill, if I remember correctly, who took care of the 40 dwellings allowing viewing and entry for measuring only. Once your bid was accepted you were given the keys with very clear instruction not to touch anything until contracts were exchanged. The very first thing I noticed was a tap in the kitchen was dripping, obviously the water main was still on and it's winter. I informed Bill immediately.

"Hi Bill, the water is still on in number one can you arrange for it to be turned off as soon as possible, it's bloody cold." I said.

"Oh, number 1 Koonowla that was the last house to be used by a Officer, I will 'phone the office to get the engineer down." He replied.

Thinking I had alerted Bill who would have 'phoned his office to request an engineer, I assumed all would be well. Returning the following week to obtain the keys from our Bill I enquired.

"Water off Bill."

"The office said they would do it right away." He replied.

He paused scratched his thinning hair and continued saying

"No bugger has been to collect any keys you better check that Joe."

Chapter Sixteen

Sure enough the water was still dripping from the tap. Back to our Bill.

"That tap is dripping Bill can you 'phone the office while I'm here so I know some action will be taken because the temperature is still dropping."
Expressing my concern by my raised voice.
He immediately picked up his 'phone and called the office.

"They will be here Monday, for sure." He said crossing his fingers.
The following week the temperature had dropped to well below zero thinking thank Christ those engineers turned off the main water supply the previous Monday, fingers crossed. The telephone rang at home.

"Hello Joe it's Bill from the M.o.D. estate, there was water coming out of your letter box, I have reported it to the office and the mains are turned off."
I was speechless for a few seconds trying not to use bad language.

"How long has it been running Bill." I asked nervously.

"Well I found it this morning on my walk round it was the noise that attracted my attention. I have no idea when the pipes burst, I'm sorry Joe."

"I'm on my way, get your manager to meet me at the house in one hour and tell him to bring a bloody big cheque book." I said in bitter anger.
Meeting the Biggin Hill estate agent at Koonowla Close, our proposed new home, we had difficulty opening the front door. The initial shock of seeing the ceilings and half the walls on the floor demoralised me. The entire lower floor was badly damaged not being able to open or close any of the internal doors due to the wood warping, even the skirting had come away from the walls, what was left of them. As our offer had been accepted by M.o.D. but contract not yet exchanged I took it I had a greater influence in any future negotiations for the damage. Arrangements were made for a meeting with the M.o.D. representatives at the premises to come to an agreement on cost of repair. A week later I met two gentleman from the M.o.D. together with the Biggin Hill estate agent and a local builder I had employed. This being my first encounter with such humans it didn't take me to long to confirm I'm dealing with Apsole's, Queens rabbits. They offered me £500 compensation for the damage, I immediately asked.

"What bloody planet do you come from, open your eyes and taker a close look at the extent of the water damage. No lower ceilings and all walls need replastering plus all the wooden fittings doors, surrounds, skirting will have to be replaced and the house will require rewiring."

"It's not that bad. Replied one rabbit.
Then my builder made it clear that all doors will have to be replaced stating the surrounds may be saved.

"Saved my arse, they've come away from what is left of the walls and I have to dry out the house before any work being carried out." I said.
I was becoming very angry with their silly offer and my builder suggesting we could save anything that had absorbed water. The atmosphere was heated as I put my foot firmly down on any offer lower that £2500. Then one rabbit stated the work could be carried out by them.

"On your bike, I wouldn't trust you to build a sand castle, You have an obligation to me and that is a reduction in the value of what is now a wreck due to your negligence after my several warnings of the potential problems." I said in a loud voice.
I was getting the better of these Queens rabbits as it went very quiet, nobody saying a word. It was me breaking the silence raising my voice.

"Come on, make up your bloody minds. I'm in trouble with a wife and two young children with no home in six weeks."
They had no idea I was in a very good financial position having a bridging loan from my employer. The cap was sealed when I suggested calling in my local MP to aid my battle with M.o.D.

"We don't have to go to that extent Mr. Merchant." Said one rabbit.

"Your right sir, we don't have to but I shall if it proves the only method to make you see your obligations to me and my family."

"We shall contact you by telephone via the agent after further discussions with our office." Said the rabbit holding the .M.o.D. pencil.

"No you bloody well will not, agreement must be now and I shall require your full cooperation on the drying out procedure that means I shall need electricity from another power point away from this very wet house. NOW,"
I shouted.
The two rabbits walked a distance away depriving us of their conversation, the mumble continued for sometime making me angrier. My builder said nothing since receiving my correction to his one and only statement. The local estate agent didn't say a word during the entire meeting knowing it was his office that caused the problem.

"Come on I don't have all day." I shouted across the room.

"Mr Merchant we can offer you £2200, plus free electricity until your move date." Turning to the estate agent he continued giving him instructions to provide power from next door.

"Mr Merchant I trust this will be to your approval and agreement as I'm sure we are all busy gentlemen."

"Yes that will be fine." I said
Pillock I thought wishing I had a couple of carrots.

Chapter Sixteen

The whole saga amazed me that these two rabbits thought they could palm me off with a pittance for reimbursement.

Back at the Swordfish bar I had an architect friend, Barry Morse, who kindly carried out an inspection on the damage and the best way to over come the drying out difficulties.

"We need to get a large dehumidifier in here as soon as possible and the windows will have to left open for a least a year. All unwanted damaged fittings, doors, skirting and damp linoleum that covered the upper floors must go" He reported.

Having hired the largest dehumidifier I could get my hands on I had to drive from Sidcup to Biggin Hill every day to empty the 5 litre water container that was collected over a 24 hour period. It took several days, with the help of a few friends, to dispose of the unwanted item and then three weeks to extract the moisture from the walls with the dehumidifier.

My employer had agreed to give us a bridging loan on the condition we had a valuation carried out on the home in Sidcup. Applying to a Sidcup estate agent making it very clear the house was not for sale. Within 20 minutes of the valuation agent leaving our home his office phoned informing me that they had somebody interested in our house. Speaking slowly I made the point.

"The - house - was - not - for - sale."

"Could we send the lady for viewing," He replied.

"You can send who you like but the house is not for sale, your job was to supply a valuation required by my employers for a bridging loan." I said.

"There is no harm in the lady looking at what is available in your area for her price range, it there? with your agreement of course." he said.

I agreed to her visit but for viewing only. The lady arrived in less than hour, making her welcome and again stipulating the house was not for sale, yet, as I wanted to sell privately due to its condition. I had maintained the entire property to a very high standard.

"I would like to buy your house, I'll give you £36,000 for it." she said.

This offer was over the top by £4,000.

"Leave your details with us and when we are in a position to move I promise to give you first refusal." I said thinking of her tempting offer. Later having contacted the lady buyer we agreed the private sales of our home in Sidcup at £35,000 exchanging contracts as soon as possible.

"No problem my Father is a solicitor, he will handle all for me," she said Three weeks before the move she reduced her offer to £33.500 and having little choice we accepted her offer. The Sidcup estate agent then sent me a bill for the introduction that I refused to pay telling them to get lost.
Moving into Koonowla Close with the help of friends and neighbours was completed in less than a day. While living on the ground floor we started on the upstairs. In total it took me 18 months and £15,000 to renovate the home into a Spanish designed interior. The woodwork was all mahogany with artext walls, it was a beautiful. By then I was so exhausted I employed a landscape company to complete the gardens. .

After several months of helping Valerie Vizer to run the Swordfish bar it was offered to us still under the ownership of Mark Campbell. We agreed to take over this small business but trying to hold down a job I hated, rebuild our home and helping to run the bar would take its toll.

Swordfish Bar Boxing Day 1980   Photo: © Pilots Pals

Fancy dress was the order of the day. P.1.G vicar - Front - Paddy Casey and David Tisard - Myself as a cowboy. At the rear is Graham Marshall as "The Incredible Hulk." Other members names have been lost with time.

Chapter 17

A dream came true living on Biggin Hill Airport with our own small business; it seemed so natural for me to be working with my friends Mark Campbell and Stuart Patterson. It was a relief to be leaving Sidcup and the hustle and bustle that attached itself to suburban life. The simple things returned giving me endless pleasures every day, walking through our village with the local people acknowledging one, a warmth one rarely finds in the cities. New ideas and opportunities appeared that would give me the freedom I had so desired.

Joseph J. Merchant 2011

Chapter Seventeen

The Swordfish bar was renamed Ark Royal after the decommissioning of the Royal Navy aircraft carrier thus maintaining a connection with the senior service. This small club was very successful and within three weeks of our take-over we had trebled the takings. More students, instructors, private owners and their friends used the club bar and it was here I would have the pleasure of meeting the members of the Papa Echo Group. This group of friends had purchased a Bolkow 209 Monsun, G-AYPE, from the distributor Air Touring Ltd. in May 1974. The enjoyment was endless with tales from John High, who became a lifelong friend, one for whom I have the utmost respect for his dedication and loyalty for all the that surrounded him. John Wright, the only Labour voter I would ever meet in my many years at Biggin Hill. Dave Turner who boasted he'd found a way to give up cigarettes saying.

"Easy, every morning I cover myself in petrol, no problem."
During a neighbours party one female guest asked David why was he a pilot, He replied.
"I find it exciting."
"Exciting, why, how?" Asked the lady.
"I'm not very good at it." Replied Dave.
He is the most humorous man and went onto become a commercial pilot flying executive aircraft based at Heathrow. The inquisitive Jim Wheeler who loved solving all sorts of problems regardless of their nature, a very interesting gentleman. Dave Buswell who sadly lost his life during an air race at Rochester in August 1984. A well respected pilot. Tony Weedon devoted his life to the Air Training Corps passing on his aviation knowledge to the young cadets. John McDermott a fun loving character who's generosity exceeded most. Dave Lawrence another of Biggin Hill's well respected instructors. Rob Tribbick who became the assistant chief designer for the BA Sea Harrier and was also involved with the BA Hawk, an interesting chap that one could listen to and never get bored. Derek Archer a very successful businessman who paid his dues but rarely flew the group's Monsun. When sharing time with these people I would reflect on the early days with 615 Squadron, the same type of fun loving characters. In my book very special people This flying group attracted outsiders that enjoyed the continuous banter. One particular character from our village was Jack the Judge, one of many, a very humorous jolly man, a magistrate who would have made a good judge, not for the accused who occupied the dock for sure as Jack was a disciplinarian and no fool. These people were just one group of great aviators that I shared my time with while running the Ark Royal.

One weekend when several of the members were discussing aerobatics a tall slim unfamiliar gentleman contributed his knowledge to the discussion making reference to the R.A.F. procedures. It was very obvious this chap knew what he was talking about, the discussion ended very quickly and he was then surrounded by the group asking questions. The unknown pilot was Sqn. Ldr. Art Legg.(Ret). who within a couple of weeks became a regular visitor to the Ark Royal bar along with his admirable wife Marnie, both became lifelong friends. There were many occasions when Art had the club members in stitches with his hilarious stories from his R.A.F. experiences. A career that started when he won a flying scholarship through his Air Training Squadron in 1958, obtaining his PPL at the Christchurch Aero Club flying Tiger Moths

Always wanting an original painting of Sqn. Ldr "Bob" Eeles Meteor I was introduced to the aviation artist Kenneth McDonough by Barry Wheeler. Ken's work had dried up from Airfix Ltd., Barry's employer. Ken agreed to the commission so work started based on my rough idea that it would include the surrounding atmosphere of R.A.F. Biggin Hill. I was a little disappointed with the result and should have been satisfied with just the original. Ken was not a jet artist, far from it, painting box covers for plastic kits did not permit the free style he would adapt later I decided to make a limited edition of 250 prints from the original work and Ken agreed to a signed edition. I tracked "Bob" down but his wife informed me that he was terribly weak with his illness. However, he agreed to sign all copies. It was during this signing visit with my friend Art Legg that it became very clear his health was deteriorating fast, a very sad visit as I had known him to be a handsome fit gentleman.

Sad Time

Sqn. Ldr Art Legg (Ret.) with Sqn. Ldr. "Bob" Eeles (Ret.) signing the first Kenneth McDonough print for my venture Circuit Publications Ltd. "Churchill's Own."

Photo: © Pilots Pals

Visits to the South East area became infrequent as most of the flying clubs and social life was now situated on the South Camp, close to what is now the entrance on Churchill Way. Very early one morning while taking the children and our dog, Brandy, for a walk we came upon our old club which brought back good memories of the days flying with the 600 Group. The shed appeared to have been used by some organisation as the window frames had been painted. So much had changed in this area. The long line of 20 plus trees that ran almost parallel with runway 29/11, trees I had come so very close to when attacking Mike Ronayne in his Tiger, G-AOBO, all now had gone.

Photo: © pilots Pals

8 am One Spring Saturday Morning 1980

The ground on the South East area was being prepared for the foundations of the Brencham hangar that was to house Mike Carlton's collection of jet fighters and executive aircraft. In the background of this image can be seen the new industrial estate; part of the Bromley Council asset stripping campaign. To my knowledge little or no money from the sale of this site came back to the airport, but the new industrial units did improve employment for the residents of Biggin Hill.

The hangar to the far right of the above image was erected and occupied by RTZ (Rio Tinto Zinc) the British Australian mining company for their Citation operation. Later it was occupied by the Racal organisation and in 1988 it was purchased by Tiphook.

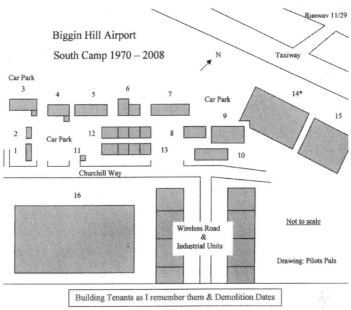

Biggin Hill Airport

South Camp 1970 – 2008

Building Tenants as I remember them & Demolition Dates

1/ Ex M.o.D. Wooden shed – Bromley Council Site Office – Mini Cab Office - 2007
2/ Ex M.o.D. Wooden Shed - 2007
3/ Ex M.o.D. R.A.F. Brick Built – J. Maitland – Scrambles Café – April 2006
4/ Flairavia Flying Club – Sword Fish/Ark Royal Bar – Mark Campbell/ Stewart
Patterson – Pilots Pals - Parachute Club – Biggin Hill Helicopter – August 2006
5/ Ex M.o.D. Brick Built 1935 – King Air Flying Club – Cabair - 2008
6/ Wooden Structure Built 1970's – First tenant unknown – Gilchrist Graphics –
Adams Aviation – Civil Air - Pilots Pals - Kent Ambulance – September 2008
7/ Ex M.o.D. Possible 1920's – Biggin Hill Flying Club – Tree Haven Trust –
King Air Flying Club - RAS Completions – August 2008
8/ Wooden Structure 1980's Experimental Flying Group – 2007
9/ Ex M.o.D. Fire Station 1935 – J. Longmoor – Transcity Exhibitions - 2008
10/ Ex M.o.D. Brick Structure Armoury 1935 – Decca – Pilots Pals – Eurotraffic –
The only Ex M.o.D. building to survive the South Camp 2008 redevelopment.
11/ Bromley Council Built Toilet 1970's - 2006
12/ Bromley Built 1970's – Civil Service Club- QS Aviation - King Air Flying Club – 1991
13/ Bromley Built 1970's - Civil Service Flying Club – Anderson Aviation - 1993 – Car Park
14/ Built by Doug Arnold for his Warbirds UK 1988 – Gold Air – Air Partners
15/ Tropair Red Hangar
16/ Built for Hunting Aviation 1993 – Formula 1.
* The unusual shape of Doug Arnold's hanger 14 will be explained later.

South Camp was the heart of Biggin Hill Airport for many years. There were a few people who created problems, known to me as Apsole's, the few being out numbered by the characters that maintained the spirit of our historic airport. It is virtually impossible to record the names of the pilots and friends who took full advantage of the fun we all shared, there were so many of us.

I was extremely proud and pleased running the "Ark Royal Bar". It provided us with additional finance to ease the cost of rebuilding our new home in Koonowla Close. The club gave me new friends from the many aviation companies that operated from Biggin Hill. Ray Notman, John Clementson and Chris Bond from Express Aviation. Peter Calvert, owner of a Rutan Verieze G-LASS, who held a record for his single engine flight from Malta to Biggin Hill and still does I believe. After his return journey I made sure that we had a great party. The Malta Air Rally was a popular event and many Biggin Hill pilots entered each year. David Gold, the former owner of Biggin Hill Flying Club, was the overall winner in both 1981 and 1982 in his Cessna 340 G-MAGS.

Photo: © Keith Sowter

Embraer EMB-110P2 Banderirante

The above Air Shetland aircraft, possibly on a maintenance flight on 18th May 1980, is unique in carrying a dual registration, the true one is the nearly unreadable G-BSVT. . The organisation Centreline operated the Banderi-ante for some years under John Willis. He introduced me to his pilots and staff, but time has blurred my memory of most of the guys and girls names. Ian Faggetter and Ed Murton are just a couple of the great bunch of characters I had the pleasure of meeting in the "Ark Royal Bar".

Sunday 21st September 1980, a very busy day at the club during the two day Air Fair. There was a buzz in the air as the many members and aircrews awaited the next event. I was standing outside with a couple of American

chaps when Don Bullock was displaying his A-26. When inverted during a barrel roll the nose of the aircraft was below the horizon, prompting one chap standing with me to say.
"Damn, he'll be lucky to pull out of that."
Within a few seconds confirmation of a disaster was evident by the orange and black plume of smoke coming from the valley. It was horrible to hear the female guests screaming. I saw Ted White walking towards the club, his head down. There was little one could say to ease the pain of those who had lost friends. I grabbed a bottle of Brandy and a few small glasses and handed to all and sundry. Peter Warren, a member, was one of the seven people lost, his female partner was in a bad way but no words could assuage her grief. Suddenly I realised my son Gary was missing thinking, *had he grabbed the opportunity to get a ride?*, my heart was pumping like a steam engine until I saw him running towards the club somewhat shaken by this disaster. Roy, our other son, was accounted for.

Photo: © Norman Rivett

Don flying his A-26 Invader N3710G

After this accident the CAA ruled that only crew would be authorised to fly in future displays, failure to comply meant ones air show authorisation licence would be revoked. Much has been written about this accident with many photographs capturing the last moments of flight. Pointing fingers had little reward or benefit to this sad loss of good people and an aircraft from the air show circuit. The following day I 'phoned Bromley Council for permission to plant 7 small trees on the bank in Oaklands Lane in the Biggin Hill Valley just short of the impact. By the following Friday the Council had done the job for me. I would put good money on the fact that my request was handled by a caring individual and not a council committee. Whoever that person was, our sincere thanks.

War Birds

Living next to the airport the sound of a Merlin made us rush to see the latest arrival. On this occasion my boys had just left their school in the village.

I came across this air to ground photo at a late stage in my writing. It shows South Camp and the Main Road prior to Bromley adding a roundabout at the entrance of Biggin Hill Airfield.

During the winter of 1980/81 I continued working for Samuel Banner as a sales representative covering South East England. But I found the job boring with little reward for my days of travelling and meeting the buyers in the surface coating industry. I found most of these buyers negative people with a very different attitude to salespeople than I had shown when purchasing for Howson Algraphy. This together with building our new home, trying to run the club and build a new business for my future left me continuously exhausted. I had made many thousands of pounds for my employers, it was now my ambition to work for myself. Thus giving me the freedom I yearned for, no accountants asking me to fill out unnecessary cost sheets and having to reply to nonsensical memos.

Thoughts of working for myself on Biggin Hill Airport would fill all my dreams. Being able to get away from the hassle that went with employment and too the political people that I disliked. From this point on I would be on my own and if trouble loomed with very few people to turn to for help. However, with a few female friends the foundations were set for the building of Pilots Pals. About which and much more you will be able to read in Volume Two; "Biggin Hill Airfield Beyond the Bump II"

THE AUTOBIOGRAPHY OF
JOSEPH J MERCHANT

BIGGIN HILL
AIRFIELD
Beyond the Bump II

Plans are to publish during 2015 in full colour with over 230 images within the 350 page book.

ISBN Number 978-0-9929626-1-6

Chapter Seventeen

Appendix a

Biggin Hill
Airfield 1994

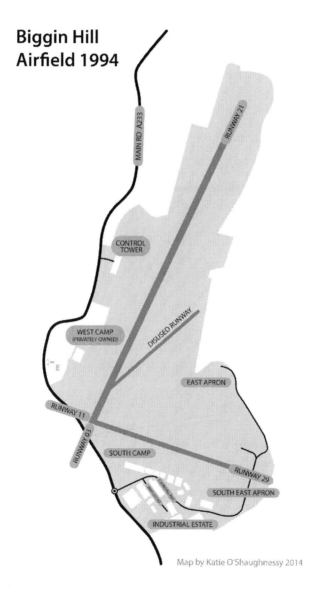

Map by Katie O'Shaughnessy 2014

Aviation Licence Abbreviations
&
Ratings

LICENCE		RATINGS
SPL	Students Pilots Licence	(Discontinued 1990's)
R.T	Radiotelephony Licence	
PPL	Private Pilots Licence	Night Rating
		I.M.C. Instrument metrological conditions
CPL	Commercial Pilots Licence	F.I. Flight Instructor
		I.R Instrument Rating
		C.F.I. Chief Flying Instructor
ATPL	Airline Transport Pilots Licence	Aircraft type rating
		T.R.I. Type Rating Instructor
		T.R.E. Type Rating Examiner